Never Kiss A Naughty Nanny

An American Farce

by

Michael Parker

SAMUEL FRENCH

FOUNDED 1830

NEW YORK HOLLYWOOD LONDON TORONTO

SAMUELFRENCH.COM

ISBN 978-0-573-65248-6   Printed in U.S.A.   #4943

IMPORTANT BILLING AND CREDIT REQUIREMENTS

NEVER KISS A NAUGHTY NANNY was first produced by Ed Fletcher Productions at the Early Bird Dinner Theatre in Clearwater, Florida on November 1st, 2007. The production was designed by Eddy Lyons & Jennifer Sloane under the direction of Robin New with the following cast:

BEN ADAMS . . . . Ian MacCallum

MR. BROADBENT . . . . Toby Manion

CASEY CODY . . . . Tracy Borgatti

MR. COTT . . . . Toby Manion

SUE JOHNSON . . . . Greta Kishbaugh

GLADYS MCNICOLL . . . . Barbara Anthony

FRED MCNICOLL . . . . Ronald Farnham

WALTER BROOKS . . . . Michael Crockett

TIME

The present.

PLACE

The "House of the Future"... Somewhere in Wisconsin.

ACT ONE: An early Friday evening in December.
ACT TWO: Later the same evening.

CHARACTERS

BEN ADAMS (age 21-30): A real estate salesman employed by Mr. Broadbent. He is young, naïve, and easily persuaded by Mr. Broadbent to pose as someone who has been living in "The House of the Future" for four years. After "The Closet of the Future" has hauled him inside, and the central trash disposal system has swallowed his pants, he comments, "I think this house has something against me personally." It certainly appears that way, as one disaster after another follows poor Ben. *(Likable, always confused and in trouble, but honest and sincere.)*

MR. BROADBENT (age 50-70): Very much a self-made man. He has fought his way up from a construction worker, to site foreman, and now owns his own home building business. His "House of the Future", however, has remained unsold for four years, probably because all the gadgets of the future fail to work properly. A brief role, which can be doubled with either Cott or Brooks. *(Blunt, rough around the edges.)*

CASEY CODY (age 20-30): Mr. Broadbent's secretary, who has been bribed by him to play the role of Ben's wife in the house of the future. She is very much the "Take charge" type. Her quick thinking saves the day on numerous occasions as she maneuvers the other characters through one disaster after another. *(Competent, resourceful, quick thinking, with a wonderful sense of humor.)*

SUE JOHNSON (age 20-25): A recent graduate of the local culinary institute hired by Mr. Broadbent to cook for Mr. and Mrs. McNicoll. We are left to wonder how she graduated from anything. She is a walking, breathing, living disaster area. She drops everything, she breaks everything, she trips over everything, she gets tangled up in everything. A charming comedic character, who spends almost the entire play without her skirt. *(Loveable, laughable, endearing.)*

MR. COTT (age 40+): The central character in the play, and he, of course, is Nanny. He is Mr. Broadbent's maintenance man, on hand in the house of the future to make running repairs on all the gadgets. He is a comedic character, who is the world's most complete hypochondriac.

You name it – he's got it! Of course the McNicoll's are not supposed to know there is a maintenance man in the house. When Mrs. McNicoll hears Casey refer to Mr. Cott, Casey quickly recovers by saying she referred to Miss Turcott, the children's nanny. SO....he spends the rest of the play as Nanny Turcott, defending his honor against the amorous advances of Mr. Brooks. *(Down to earth, gruff, but very, very funny.)*

GLADYS MCNICOLL (age 40+): The perspective buyer of the house of the future. She totally dominates her poor hen-pecked husband, and indeed all those around her. She is a thoroughly distasteful unlikable woman, with few, if any, redeeming qualities. *(Loud, aggressive, overbearing.)*

FRED MCNICOLL (age 40+): The poor hen-pecked husband of Gladys. He is rarely allowed to have a thought of his own, finish a sentence, or do anything without being criticized by Gladys. Audiences, however, sympathize with him and rejoice when he has his "Moment in the sun", and turns the table on Gladys at the very end of the play. *(Meek, mild, good-natured, and finally in control.)*

WALTER BROOKS (age 40+): A surprise visitor whose car has got stuck in a snowdrift, and who has to spend the night in the house. He develops an almost insane infatuation for Nanny, and will not be discouraged. His relentless pursuit of Nanny lands him in many of the physical comedic sequences. *(Bull headed, single minded, not very likable.)*

ACT 1

The curtain rises on an empty set. It is the living room and kitchen of a very strange looking house. Built some years previously by Mr. Broadbent, a developer and building contractor, as "The House of the Future," it has nevertheless remained unsold. It has not only been a huge white elephant for Mr. Broadbent, but has become the laughing stock of the industry in this part of Wisconsin. This is probably because, as we shall see, most of the gadgets and innovations of the future fail to work properly.

D.R. is a large front door, and above it, on the R. wall is a narrow louvered door to "The Closet of the Future." U.R. is the kitchen with a counter and two stools. There is a pepper-mill on the counter. The back wall of the kitchen consists of cabinets, which extend off R. The R. wall of the kitchen is open, leading to the rest of the house. The cabinets on the rear wall end L. with a large refrigerator. Immediately to the L. of the fridge is a strange looking structure. It is the ion chamber. It can be round or square, about seven feet high, and just big enough for a single person to be inside when the door is closed. It should be made to look metallic with some kind of visible locking device on the outside. To the L. of the kitchen counter is another tubular shaped object, which is attached to the counter by an "arm." It is about one foot in diameter and about three feet high. It looks a little like a round stool. It is part of the central vacuum system. [SEE AUTHOR'S NOTES FOR ALL THE "HOUSE OF THE FUTURE" INNOVATIONS]

Hanging down from the kitchen counter is a fabric sign with "HAPPY BIRTHDAY" written on it There are other decorations including several groups of balloons attached to the walls with colored ribbons. D.L. is a large stone fireplace with a small vase of flowers on the mantle. Against the L. wall above the fireplace is a couch with two small cushions and an afghan. To the L. of the couch, is a wall-mounted lamp. Above the couch on the L. wall is the door to bedroom 1. In front of the couch is a low coffee table and to its R. a low back easy chair. U.L. is an open archway leading to the master bedroom.

On the U.S. wall are two doors. R. is the bathroom, and L. is bedroom 2. Between bedroom 2 and the bathroom is a face-plate with two switches. Directly above the bathroom door is light fixture with a red bulb. R. of the bathroom door is the bathroom cleaning switch.

After a few moments **BEN ADAMS** *enters from off R. in the kitchen. He is a clean-cut young man, age perhaps 25-30. He is a gentle, mild mannered soul, usually dominated by the more forceful personalities of those around him. He is dressed smartly, but casually in a sport jacket, dress pants and shoes, but no tie. As he crosses in front of the fridge, the front door bell chimes and the fridge door swings open, hitting* **BEN** *and almost knocking him down. As he gets up the chimes continue at a rapid pace and only stop when he closes the fridge door. He looks at it for a second, then at the front door. He tentatively opens the fridge door and the chimes start up again. He closes it, they stop. He opens it, they start, he closes it again, they stop. There is now a loud knocking on the front door, so* **BEN** *hurries D.R. and unlocks the door. As he opens the door there is a bang from the fireplace, which then lights up.* **BEN** *looks L. very bewildered.*

MR. BROADBENT *steps into the room. He is middle aged, and appears to be very much a self-made man. He has fought his way up from a construction worker, to a site foreman, and now owns his own business. He is wearing a business suit with a bulky overcoat, hat, scarf and gloves. He is carrying a large cardboard box which he puts down just inside the front door.*

BROADBENT. What took you so long Ben? It's freezing out there. (*Closes the door*)

BEN. I'm sorry Mr. Broadbent, but when you rang the doorbell, the fridge sort of attacked me.

BROADBENT. Oh Lord! It's the wiring on the remote dooropeners that's all screwed up. Anyway, I've got Ed Cott from the maintenance department on his way over here, he'll be able to fix it. What was that noise?

BEN. Well, when I opened the front door, there was this bang in the fireplace.

BROADBENT. Ah, yes. We've always had trouble with that. It's the wiring on the self-lighting fireplace. It seems to have got connected to the front door somehow. Remind me to get Cott to fix it.

BEN. Mr. Broadbent, may I have a word with you.

BROADBENT. Of course Ben, why not be a devil and have two, why not go completely wild and try a whole sentence?

BEN. Well, I know I work for you, but I'm supposed to be a salesman and sell the houses you build, and I'm very nervous about your plan for this weekend.

BROADBENT. Look Ben, you're a real estate salesman, this house is a piece of real estate and this weekend we're going to sell it.

BEN. I know that's what you said but –

BROADBENT. (*Takes off his hat, gloves, scarf and overcoat*) Listen to me my boy. I built this house four years ago as "The House of the Future." It was my baby, by brainchild. I put my heart and soul into this place, not to mention nearly three hundred thousand dollars. It was supposed to be the first of a whole new series of homes, with a whole new concept of modern living. Here, let me show you. Let me just get a remote.

(*He reaches into the cardboard box and produces an instrument that looks like a T.V. remote*)

Watch this. Now, in an ordinary house I'd have to open a closet door to put my coat away, but not here my boy.

All I have to do is press the right number here, or you can use that switch right there,

(*He points to the switch on the wall above the front door. Then he clicks the remote, the closet door slides open*)

and here you have the "Closet of the Future"

(*An artificial human arm appears at about shoulder height and moves about 3 feet into the room. It has a hand on the end of it with only the middle finger sticking out horizontal to the ground*)

and what's more, you can lower the height of it for children.

(*He puts his coat, scarf, and gloves on the arm, pauses for a second and frowns at "the finger," then covers it with his hat. He clicks the remote again, the arm withdraws and the closet door slides silently shut.*)

What do you think of that?

BEN. That's incredible.

BROADBENT. That's nothing. Look at this.

(*He goes up to the ion chamber and opens the door.*)

This is a personal ion chamber. It works on compressed air just like the closet.

BEN. What does it do?

BROADBENT. Well, You know about these ion exchangers they have for softening water?

BEN. Vaguely.

BROADBENT. O.K. It shoots these charged particles at you and relaxes all your muscles. Women love it. It makes their hair all soft and manageable. Do you want to try it?

BEN. Well sir, everyone at the office tells me nothing works properly in this house. Isn't it a bit dangerous?

BROADBENT. Not at all. We had one or two teething problems, but everything works fine now. Go on. Get in. It'll be fine.

BEN. Well, if you're sure it's O.K.

(*The front door bell rings, and the fridge door opens to hit* **BEN** *who falls to the ground. The chimes continue rapidly until* **MR. BROADBENT** *closes the fridge door, then they stop. He gives the front door a puzzled look, then opens the fridge a fraction. The chimes start again,* **BEN** *gets to his feet and watches* **MR. BROADBENT** *close the door, the chimes stop. He opens it they start. He closes it, they stop.*)

BROADBENT. (*Heads D.R. to the front door*) That'll be my secretary Casey. She left the office at the same time I did.

(*He opens the front door – The fire place does its bang, and light up routine.* **CASEY CODY** *steps into the room, as* **BROADBENT** *closes the door.* **CASEY** *is young and pretty, age perhaps 25-30, she is very confident in her manner and bearing. She will prove herself to be very much the "take charge type." She is wearing a skirt, sweater, boots and a long winter coat with a woolen ski cap. She carries a small overnight case which she puts down by the counter, takes off her hat and shakes her hair loose.*)

Come in Casey. I'm glad you're here.

CASEY. I'm glad I'm here too. It's miserable out there. It's starting to snow again.

BEN. Hi Casey.

CASEY. Hi Ben.

BROADBENT. I was just showing Ben some of the features of the house of the future, and you'll need to know how everything works as well.

(**CASEY** *has taken her coat off*)

Here, let me introduce you to the closet of the future.

(*He clicks his remote and the closet door slides open, but this time the arm appears moving ever so slowly. He takes Casey's coat and hangs it on the hand*)

Oh dear, that's a bit slow. I guess the air system needs topping off. Never mind, Cott'll fix that when he gets here.

(*The arm moves slowly back into the closet as* **BEN** *and* **CASEY** *look knowingly at each other*)

O.K., now pay attention you two. Here's the plan.

(*He paces across the room as* **BEN** *and* **CASEY** *sit on the two stools at the kitchen counter*)

I've decided the reason this house has never sold is because people are afraid of all the gadgets and appliances. Now, I've got this couple who seemed really interested when I told them about the house. Their name is McNicoll. To-day is Mrs. McNicoll's birthday and I've invited them to spend tonight in this house, and we are going to wine and dine them. They are going to see what a wonderful house this is, and you two are going to show them how well everything works.

(*He's now "on a roll" and pacing rapidly*)

I want them to believe that you two have been living here renting the house. I do not want them to know it's been empty for four years.

BEN. Isn't that dishonest sir?

BROADBENT. (*Frowns at* **BEN**) Not at all. I just want to create an opportunity to show them all the features.

BEN. You mean you want Casey and I to pretend we're married.

BROADBENT. Exactly

BEN. I'm not sure I'm very good at that sort of thing.

CASEY. Oh come on Ben! We can pull it off.

BROADBENT. Don't forget you both get a five thousand dollar bonus if it sells, and incidentally so does Cott.

BEN. But what if the gadgets go wrong? They always seem to.

BROADBENT. I've got that covered. Cott will be here shortly, he was involved in the construction of the house. He'll stay all weekend and be available to make running repairs if anything goes wrong.

CASEY. Won't Mr. and Mrs. McNicoll think it's a bit odd if there's a maintenance man here all the time?

BROADBENT. Hmm. You're right, he'd better keep in the background, we won't ever let the McNicolls see him.

BEN. We?

BROADBENT. Well, you two.

BEN. Where will you be?

BROADBENT. I'm going home.

BEN. Oh dear, I'm sure something will go wrong.

CASEY. For five thousand dollars, I'm going to make sure nothing does.

BROADBENT. O.K. Let's get moving. Let me introduce you to the house of the future.

(*He picks up the cardboard box he brought with him and puts it on the L. end of the kitchen counter*)

I don't have time to go over everything, but here's a bunch of brochures we printed about the house.

(*He takes them out of the box and hands them to* **CASEY** *who keeps one in her hand and puts the others on the counter.*)

Here are all the remotes I could round up.

(*He puts four remotes on the counter*)

You can work just about everything in the house with these. You just look up the number in the brochure. Here let me show you. Ben I believe you were going to try the ion chamber

BEN. Are you sure it'll work?

(**BROADBENT** *gives him a "look"*)

O.K., O.K.

(*He gets in,* **BROADBENT** *closes the door and clicks the remote.*)

CASEY. (*Who has been looking at the brochure*) What's this about a self-cleaning bathroom?

BROADBENT. That's the bathroom for this bedroom. That's the door there. See that switch just to the left, that automatically seals the door shut and then floods the whole room with jet sprays to clean it. Kind of like a laser car wash.

CASEY. What happens if someone is in there?

BROADBENT. That's why the switch is outside the door and not on the remote. The second you hit the switch the door locks so you can't get in. A red light above the door flashes while it's spraying, and a buzzer sounds when it's finished.

(**BEN** *re-appears from the ion chamber, leaving the door open*)

Well what do you think?

BEN. I don't think it does anything.

BROADBENT. The compressed air system probably needs recharging. Just make sure Cott tops it off when he gets here.

(*A phone rings.* **BEN** *and* **CASEY** *look around, but can't see a phone.* **MR. BROADBENT** *grins at them and crosses D.L. to the fireplace. He moves the vase on the mantle a little clockwise. The ringing stops as he leans closer to it and talks.*)

Hello. Oh, hi. What? O.K. Look, do me a favor will you? Stop by the office and pick up a Miss Susan Johnson. It'll save me a trip. Thanks. (*He turns the vase back*)

CASEY. He's talking to a vase!

BROADBENT. This is the house of the future. We don't have phones that look like phones. There are five or six of them in this room. This vase is one of them. I can't remember where they all are. Casey, you've got the brochure.

(**CASEY** *studies it*)

BEN. But what's the point?

BROADBENT. What do you mean, what's the point?

BEN. What's wrong with a telephone?

BROADBENT. You have no imagination my boy. The point is we've got all these phones and don't have a single ugly piece of plastic to look at.

CASEY. You know, that actually makes sense. (*Looking at the brochure*) It says here that switch next to the bathroom door is one.

BROADBENT. O.K. That was Cott a minute ago on the phone. He's running a little late, says it's snowing real hard. Anyway, what I didn't tell you is that I've hired a gal from the culinary institute. She's going to cook and serve a gourmet meal tonight for Mr. and Mrs. McNicoll. There's also some expensive wine in the fridge.

BEN. You're really laying it on aren't you?

BROADBENT. You betcha. I've had too much money tied up in this place for too long. This is my big chance to get out from under. O.K. It's almost six-thirty and they're invited for seven, so, study the brochure and be sure to tell Cott to re-charge the air system as soon as he gets here.

BEN. How do you make a call?

BROADBENT. What?

BEN. How do you dial out if you want to make a phone call?

BROADBENT. It's voice activated. You just turn the vase or whatever it is you do to the other things and say the number. It's an intercom as well. You just open the line and say the number of the extension. You know, one, two, three or four et cetera and it rings in the appropriate place. It's all in the brochure.

BEN. I'm very nervous about pretending to be married. I think you're asking a bit much.

BROADBENT. Is five thousand dollars too much?

CASEY. He's got a point.

BROADBENT. (*Clicks his remote and moves D.R. to the closet. The closet works as before, but painfully slowly, and this time the index finger sticks up in the classic "finger" pose.*) We've got to get the McNicoll's in a festive mood. Remember now, I'm counting on you. You got a sales contract Ben?

BEN. Of course.

BROADBENT. Good, have it ready. Right after dinner and wine should be a good time. Remember now, make sure Mrs. McNicoll has a good time on her birthday.

(*He takes his hat, coat and scarf from "The Finger" and puts them on. He clicks again and looks at "The Finger" as it moves slowly back into the closet*)

You know, I don't know what it is, but there's something about that hand that's just not right.

CASEY. Can't quite put your finger on it, eh?

BROADBENT. Ah well, I'm outa here.

BEN. Where are we going to sleep?

BROADBENT. Well, you two are supposed to be living here, so you'll have to have the master bedroom. Put Mr. and Mrs. McNicoll in this room. (*He indicates bedroom 2.*) That way they can use the self-cleaning bathroom. Any other problems?

BEN. I guess not.

BROADBENT. O.K. Good luck, see you tomorrow.

(*He exits the front door. The fireplace does its bang routine.*)

BEN. (*Jumps*) Can't we stop it doing that? Maybe Cott will fix it when he gets here.

CASEY. (*Who has been reading the brochure.*) That peppermill on the counter is another phone. It's number four, (*She goes behind the counter*) and that switch in the ion chamber is another one, it's number two. (*She twists the peppermill and speaks into it.*) Number two. (*The switch in the ion chamber rings*) Go on. Answer it.

BEN. (*Enters the ion chamber and flips the switch*) Hello.

CASEY. That's wild. I can hear you.

BEN. I don't suppose it's occurred to you that we're standing about six feet from each other, and don't need a phone.

CASEY. Well, yes, between these two phones, but I might be somewhere else in the house. (*Puts the peppermill down*)

BEN. I guess. (*Flips the switch, steps out of the chamber, and closes the door*)

CASEY. Look, cheer up Ben, life can't be that bad, and for five thousand bucks each I think we should give it our best shot.

BEN. I'm sorry Casey. You're right.

CASEY. (*Picks up her case, and still carrying the brochure, heads L. toward the master bedroom.*) O.K. I'm going to put my things away.

BEN. Where are we going to sleep?

CASEY. Mr. Broadbent just told you. We –

BEN. No, no. I meant, where are you and I going to sleep. There's just one bed in there.

CASEY. (*Stops and turns*) Don't you think I'm the one who ought to be worrying about that. I'm engaged and if my fiancé knew I was here pretending to be married and sharing a room with you, he'd have a heart attack.

BEN. Well, what do you think we should do?

CASEY. Tell you what, after Mr. and Mrs. McNicoll have gone to bed, one of us will move into another bedroom. O.K?

She exits U.L. as the front door chimes start. **BEN** *leaps away from the fridge door and just avoids being hit as it opens. He closes the fridge door and the chimes stop. He goes D.R. to the front door and opens it. The fireplace does its usual bang routine.* **SUSAN JOHNSON** *steps into the room followed by* **MR. COTT.** *They are both brushing snow off themselves.* **BEN** *quickly closes the front door.* **SUSAN** *is young, perhaps about 25, and very pretty. She is wearing snow boots, a full length winter coat, scarf and knitted ski hat. She is carrying a large cardboard box.*

She is followed by **MR. COTT**, *age 55-65. He has definitely seen better days. He is a chronic complainer, and, as we shall see, does not seem to have much enthusiasm for life in general, and in particular for "The House of*

*the Future." He's wearing a heavy overcoat, over a denim
work shirt, blue jeans, work boots and a baseball cap. He
is also carrying a large cardboard box.*

COTT. Hi Ben.

BEN. Hi Eddie.

COTT. Mr. Cott to you young man. Well, don't just stand
there, be a gentleman and help the lady.

BEN. Oh, of course.

(*As he reaches for the box,* **SUE** *just lets go of it and it
drops to the floor*)

SUE. Oh dear, I'm sorry.

COTT. (*Puts his box on the kitchen counter*) You know I'm too
old to be carrying loads like this. It's bad for my back.

BEN. (*Picking up Sue's box and putting it on the counter*) I hope
nothing got broken.

SUE. It'll be alright, it's just food.

BEN. Oh, I suppose I should introduce myself. I'm Ben
Adams.

SUE. Hi. I'm Sue Johnson

BEN. Oh, you're the cook.

SUE. (*Taking off her hat*) Chef actually, but that's alright.

BEN. Let me take your coat.

(*He goes to hold her coat from behind, and* **SUE** *drops
her hat on the floor. As she pulls her first arm out of the
coat, the sleeve is pulled inside out. She reaches to pull it
right side in with her other arm, which is still in the coat
sleeve. Not only does this not work, but it also forces* **BEN**
to let go of the coat.)

Let me get it.

(*He reaches into the sleeve,* **SUE** *turns and they both
end up twisted together, each with one arm in the coat.
After a variety of contortions, the coat comes free.* **SUE** *is
wearing a "Slim line" wrap around skirt and a bulky
turtle-neck sweater.* **BEN,** *who is now holding the coat,
presses the closet button on the wall. "The arm" appears*

*as before, but this time in really slow motion, with the
finger returned to its horizontal position.)*

Oh, that reminds me, Mr. Broadbent told me to tell
you to top off the compressed air system.

*(He puts Sue's coat and scarf on the arm, picks up her
hat and puts it on the finger then presses the button
again. The arm very slowly returns to the closet and the
door closes.)*

COTT. Looks like it needs a major overhaul to me. Still, I
suppose more air pressure can't hurt. I'll get my cylinder. I'll be right back.

(Exit front door, the fireplace does its bang routine.)

SUE. *(Closes the front door behind* COTT.*)* It's really snowing
hard now.

BEN. Well, fortunately the heating system seems to be the
only thing that works around here.

SUE. Mr. Broadbent told me all about the house of the
future. It sounds terrific.

BEN. I wouldn't get too excited if I were you, it's full of
crazy ideas. Very few of which seem to work.

SUE. Well, I've been hired to cook and serve a gourmet
meal for a Mr. and Mrs. McNicoll, so as long as I've got
a kitchen, I'm O.K. *(She wanders off R. into the kitchen)*
Oh, it looks wonderful. *(Re-appears)* By the way, what
are you doing here?

BEN. Well, I'm supposed to be renting this house so Casey
and I, she's my wife, I mean she's not really my wife,
just for today, that is, not really, I mean a proper wife.
I'm really a salesman, and Casey's a secretary, we don't
know how anything works and I'm really nervous about
who's sleeping where.

SUE. *(Taking things out of the box and putting them on the counter off R.)* You sound a little confused.

BEN. Oh, I'm always confused.

SUE. I'm sure everything will work out. *(Still unloading groceries, etc.)* Are you really married?

BEN. Oh no!

SUE. Why "Oh no!"

BEN. What do you mean?

SUE. Why "Oh no," why not just "no"?

BEN. I don't know, I just don't think I'm ready for marriage.

SUE. Really?

BEN. I don't think I understand women. I mean, why are single women always looking for husbands, and married women always seem to be trying to get rid of theirs?

SUE. (*Comes L. a little and gives him a little kiss on the cheek*) Well, I think you're cute.

CASEY (*Enters from U.L. and crosses R. She still has a brochure in her hand*). Hi, I'm Casey, Mr. Broadbent's secretary and Ben's wife for the weekend.

SUE. Hi. I'm Sue Johnson. I'm the chef Mr. Broadbent hired.

CASEY. Did he also hire you to kiss Ben?

BEN. She didn't really kiss me.

CASEY. Why, Ben Adams, I do believe you're blushing.

SUE. Why don't I get the rest of my stuff organized.

(*As she exits R. behind the counter, she gives* **BEN** *a little pinch on the buns*)

BEN. Ooh!

CASEY. What?

BEN. (*Looking wistfully after* **SUE**) Oh nothing.

CASEY. O.K. Lets get organized. Where's Cott?

BEN. He went to get an air cylinder.

SUE. (*Off in the kitchen there is a crash of a plate as it breaks on the floor*) Oops.

(*Sue enters holding two pieces of the broken plate*)

Never mind, there's lots more. Where's the trash can?

(*They all look around*)

CASEY. Hold on, let me look. (*She thumbs through the brochure*) It says here the house has a central trash disposal system and this (*She points to the round object at the end of the counter*) is it.

SUE. I wonder how it works.

BEN. I wonder if it works.

CASEY. It doesn't tell you where to switch it on. Wait a minute, here we are. It says just hold the trash somewhere near it and it'll just suck it right in.

SUE. O.K.

(*She holds a large piece of plate above the unit and lets it go. It falls straight down and breaks on the floor. SUE just stands there*)

CASEY. Maybe it needs air too.

BEN. (*Picking up the pieces*) Or maybe you have to activate it with the remote.

CASEY. (*Looking at the brochure*) That's a point. That's it. Number twenty-seven. Here we go.

(**BEN**, *who has been bending down picking up broken pieces, is right by the trash cylinder as* **CASEY** *punches the remote. There is a whining sound and Ben's hands are sucked down the top of the cylinder.*)

BEN. Whoa! Switch it off. It's too strong.

(**CASEY** *punches buttons, the noise stops and* **BEN** *straightens up*)

Boy oh boy! Someone tell Cott this has too much air pressure.

SUE. Did you say number twenty-seven?

CASEY. Yes.

SUE. Right, that's one number I'd better remember.

(*Enter* **COTT** *through the front door. The fireplace does its bang routine. He's carrying a compressed air cylinder, which he puts down just inside the door.*)

COTT. That's strange. (*He closes, then opens the front door. The bang routine is repeated.*) That's the first time that's ever worked properly.

BEN. That's how it's supposed to work?

COTT. Well, it's a bit loud, but at least it's working. Ben, be a good lad and put this cylinder in the control room for me.

(**BEN** *comes D.R. and picks it up, then exits off R. in the kitchen followed by* **COTT**)

I'd carry it myself, but I had this double hernia a while back and carrying loads like that puts pressure on my kidneys, and then on top of that there's my gall stones –

(*Exit R. to kitchen*)

SUE. (*Behind the counter unpacking groceries*) How long have you worked for Mr. Broadbent?

CASEY. Oh, about three years. How about you, what do you do?

SUE. Well, I don't really do anything yet. I just graduated from the culinary institute, so I'm looking for a job.

CASEY. You must be a good chef for Mr. Broadbent to hire you, and you're a lucky girl as well. How, in heavens name, do you keep that figure working with food all day?

SUE. Well, in high school I had this terrific exercise called shooting the putt, no, that's not it, putting the shoot, no that's not it either. I know, it was called shot-putt.

CASEY. You don't look like a shot-putter to me.

SUE. Well, I only did it for a little while. You see you have to throw these steel balls out of a circle, but I kept running out of balls and it just got too expensive.

CASEY. I see. You did graduate didn't you?

SUE. Oh yes, but I did miss the graduation ceremony.

CASEY. Why was that?

SUE. I got on the wrong bus, and ended up in Milwaukee.

CASEY. Oh dear.

BEN. (*Enters from the kitchen and heads straight D.R. to the closet*) O.K., Cott says he's fixed the air pressure in the closet, so lets give it a try.

(*He flips the switch and the arm moves out ever so slowly until it is right next to* **BEN**'s *shoulder, then very suddenly and very fast the finger hooks in his armpit and drags him quickly into the closet.*)

Oh, Oh, Oh!

(*The door closes.*)

CASEY. (*Looking at the brochure*) I don't think it's supposed to do that.

(**BEN** *is heard yelling for help*)

Sue, can you get Cott in here please.

SUE. O.K. (*Exit R. in the kitchen*)

CASEY. (*Moves cautiously down towards the closet*) Oh dear, are you alright Ben?

(*Muffled sounds from the closet*)

Hold on, I'm going to open it again.

(*She clicks the switch and stands back. The door opens and the arm, now in the middle of* **BEN**'s *shoulder blades, pushes him into the room very fast. He collapses on the floor. The arm returns and the door closes.* **CASEY** *helps him up*)

Are you alright?

BEN. I'm beginning to think this house has got something against me personally.

(*Enter* **COTT** *and* **SUE** *from the kitchen.* **COTT** *has now removed his coat and is wearing a blue denim shirt, and blue jeans with a tool belt*).

CASEY. The closet seems to be acting up. Can you do anything?

COTT. Well, I just topped off the air, it should be O.K. now.

BEN. I think maybe it's got too much air.

COTT. That's possible. I'll go and check the pressure in a minute. I topped off the ion chamber as well. I need one of you to test it.

BEN. Well don't look at me. I'm not going in that thing again. Anyway, why don't you test it yourself. You're getting a bonus as well as us.

COTT. You've got to be kidding. Not even for five thousand dollars, and anyway, I've got a chronic embolism, any sudden movement and I could go just like that. (*Snaps fingers*)

SUE. Ooh – could I try it?

COTT. Be my guest.

(*He opens the door and* **SUE** *gets in closing the door.* **CASEY** *hands* **COTT** *her remote, which he clicks.*)

I would test it you know, but I just can't take the chance. You see I have this nervous condition, and the doctor says if I'm subjected to any stress at all it could trigger a massive heart attack.

CASEY. Don't you think – – – (*but* **COTT** *is on a roll.*)

COTT. But that's not the half of it. The real problem is the discs in my lower back which –

CASEY. (*Laughs.*) Don't you think its could all be psycho-somatic?

COTT. What does that mean?

CASEY. You know all in your head.

COTT. No, there's nothing up there, it's all down here. (*Points to his lower back.*)

CASEY. You said it, not me!

(*The ion chamber door opens to reveal* **SUE**. *Her skirt is round her ankles, and her hair is sticking straight up in the air. She staggers out and collapses momentarily behind the kitchen counter.* (*SEE AUTHOR'S NOTES.*) **COTT** *helps her up, her hair is now normal and she pulls up the skirt.*)

COTT. Are you alright Miss?

SUE. I guess so, that kind of took me by surprise.

CASEY. What happened?

COTT. It looks like it's got too much pressure at the bottom and not enough at the top. I'll try to adjust it, back in a minute. (*Exit R. in the kitchen*)

BEN. You sure you're O.K.?

SUE. I'm fine, but thanks for asking. What's this five thousand dollars he was talking about?

BEN. Oh, we all get a bonus if we sell the house this weekend. Tell you what. Why don't I help you in the kitchen?

SUE. Thank you, that's very sweet of you. (*She smiles and touches his cheek*) I think I'd like that Ben.

(*They exit R. in the kitchen*)

(**CASEY** *standing by the fridge door, watches them go as the front door bell chimes. The fridge door opens and hits her, she goes down, the chimes continue as she gets up and closes the fridge door. The chimes stop. She looks at the front door and then at the fridge. She opens the fridge, the chimes start, she closes it, they stop. She opens it, they start*)

BEN. (*Enters from the kitchen*) Casey, there's someone at the door.

CASEY. Have you noticed when you close the fridge door –

(*She closes it and the chimes stop*)

BEN. (*Moving D.R. to the front door*) Yes, I know. We need to get Cott to disconnect it. (*He opens the front door, the fireplace does its usual bang*) Come in, come in.

(*Enter* **GLADYS** *and* **FRED MCNICOLL.** **GLADYS** *is a large woman who, as we shall see, dominates her poor hen-pecked husband. She is best described as an "old battleaxe." She is wearing boots, gloves, scarf, etc., and a long winter coat over a dowdy, dark colored dress. She has no jewelry or accessories. She carries a rolled umbrella. She is followed by her husband,* **FRED,** *a small, shy, bespectacled man, who has suffered in silence for many years the overbearing attitude and aggressive manner of his wife. He is wearing an overcoat, hat, gloves, etc. over a conservative business suit, shirt and tie. He is* *carrying two large suitcases, which he puts down just inside the front door. Both he and* **GLADYS** *are brushing snow off themselves.*)

CASEY. (*Comes D.R. as* **BEN** *closes the door*) Hi, I'm Casey Cody. You must be Fred and Gladys McNicoll. Welcome to the house of the future.

GLADYS. Who are you? What are you doing here?

CASEY. Well, I – er – I live here.

GLADYS. (*Wandering L. across the room, prodding cushions with her umbrella and checking for dust everywhere with her finger*) What do you mean, you live here? Mr. Broadbent said this house was for sale.

CASEY. Oh yes, it is. My husband (*She looks knowingly at* **BEN**) and I are just renting it.

GLADYS. Renting it! I'm not sure we want to buy a house that's been rented. What do you think Fred?

FRED. Well, I –

GLADYS. Rental houses indeed. What does that tell you about the neighborhood Fred?

FRED. That the local deli doesn't have valet parking?

GLADYS. There was an innuendo in that remark Fred. I've told you I don't like these obtrusive comments. It might be alright I suppose, (*Turns to* **BEN**.) and who are you?

CASEY. He's my husband, Ben Adams.

GLADYS. I see. How do you do?

(*She shakes hands with* **BEN**.)

Fred!

(*Her look commands* **FRED** *to shake hands*)

BEN. How do you do?

FRED. Hello

GLADYS. Wait a minute, I thought you said your name was Casey Cody.

CASEY. Well, it is. Er – Casey Cody Adams. (**GLADYS** *looks blank*) Er – Cody was my maiden name.

GLADYS. I see, what do you think of that Fred?

FRED. Well, actually I think –

GLADYS. Try not to think Fred. Now, where is our room?

CASEY. You'll be right here, next to the bathroom of the future.

GLADYS. Good. Now where's that ion chamber Mr. Broadbent told me about?

BEN. (*Points to it*) It's right here.

GLADYS. Fred would like to try it, wouldn't you Fred?

FRED. Well, actually –

CASEY. You can't use it right now.

GLADYS. Why not?

CASEY. It's – er – it needs cleaning.

GLADYS. Not clean! What do you think of that Fred?

FRED. Well actually –

CASEY. Well – er – I – er – we were just in the middle of cleaning it. Weren't we Ben?

BEN. We were?

GLADYS. Good, we like clean, don't we Fred?

FRED. Oh yes dear. Er – Gladys dear, don't you think it was very nice of these people to wish you a happy birthday.

GLADYS. What!

FRED. The sign dear.

GLADYS. Oh yes.

FRED. Do you suppose we should say thank you?

GLADYS. Are you telling me what to do?

FRED. No dear.

GLADYS. Good.

CASEY. Now, before you go to your room we should give each of you a remote and one of these brochures so that –

GLADYS. Just give them to Fred. He'll be in charge of all the gadgets.

BEN. O.K. Here you are Fred.

(*He gets a remote and a brochure from the kitchen counter and hands them to* **FRED**.)

Let me show you how it works. Now, let's say you want to hang your coats up. Look in the brochure under closet and you'll see number twelve. Go on, press 12.

(**FRED** *looks questioningly at* **GLADYS** *who gives him a nod of approval, so he clicks the remote. They watch as the closet works perfectly*)

GLADYS. Isn't that wonderful. What do you think of that Fred?

FRED. Well actually –

GLADYS. Don't just stand there, take my coat.

FRED. Yes dear.

(*He takes her coat, hat, gloves, umbrella, etc. and hangs them on the closet rail as* **GLADYS** *wanders L. again checking for dust, looking behind cushions etc.* **FRED** *then hangs up his own hat and coat.*)

BEN. It actually worked.

CASEY. Shh!

GLADYS. (*Doesn't miss a beat*) Though I really don't need an automatic closet.

CASEY. Why not?

GLADYS. Well, I've got Fred. Haven't I dear?

FRED. Haven't you what?

GLADYS. Do pay attention Fred.

FRED. I'm sorry I –

GLADYS. Never mind. Fred, I want you to study that brochure and memorize all the numbers so you can work the remote for me.

FRED. Very well dear. Shall I close the closet now?

GLADYS. Yes, go ahead.

(**FRED** *clicks the remote, the closet slides back into the wall and the door closes.*)

Now, let's get to our room.

There is a loud crash in the kitchen and SUE enters with pieces of broken dishes in her hands.

SUE. Oh, hello.

GLADYS. Who are you?

SUE. I'm Sue

GLADYS. Sue who?

SUE. Sue the chef.

GLADYS. Sue Le-chef? Are you French?

SUE. No, but I nearly got to France once.

GLADYS. What do you mean? How can you nearly get to France?

SUE. Well, I had it all planned. I had my airplane ticket from Chicago to Paris, but I missed the plane.

GLADYS. What?

SUE. You see, I got on the wrong bus, and ended up in Milwaukee.

GLADYS. That's all very interesting I'm sure, but you haven't told me what you're doing here.

SUE. I'm here to cook for you this evening.

GLADYS. Fred doesn't like rich food, do you Fred?

FRED. Well, actually –

GLADYS. It gives him heartburn, doesn't it Fred?

FRED. Yes dear.

SUE. I'll remember that.

CASEY. Here, I'll show you to your room.

(*She exits to bedroom 2, followed by GLADYS, followed by FRED carrying the two suitcases*)

BEN. How can he stand living with that woman?

SUE. She is a bit much isn't she?

BEN. A bit much? She's the greatest living argument for euthanasia I've ever seen. (*He points to the dish in Sue's hands*) Another one, huh?

SUE. I'm afraid so.

BEN. (*Opens the fridge door and bends down to look inside*) Want a drink or something?

SUE. No thanks, I just came to get rid of this dish. Oh, I know. (*She picks up the last remote on the counter*) Number twenty-seven.

(*She clicks the remote, we hear the sucking noise and she drops the pieces of the broken dish in the cylinder. She exits R. into the kitchen leaving the remote at the extreme R. end of the counter as* **BEN**'s *derriere is sucked backwards onto the cylinder*)

BEN. AIEOOW! (*He contorts and wriggles, but he is unable to stand up*) Ow – Ow – Ow! (*He tries to reach the remote, but it is just out of reach*) Sue!

(**CASEY, GLADYS** *and* **FRED**, *hearing the noise, appear from BEDROOM 2, to watch his contortions. He does not see them.*)

GLADYS. Is your husband always like that?

CASEY. Like what?

GLADYS. Well, look at him. He looks like he's having an argument with his underwear.

CASEY. Ah – well – yes – you see – er – er – he has this disease.

GLADYS. I hope it's not catching.

CASEY. No, no, not at all.

GLADYS. Well, what is it? He looks like he's doing a lap dance.

CASEY. It's – er – that's it. Saint Vitas Dance.

GLADYS. Oh dear, I've heard of that.

CASEY. You have?

GLADYS. Yes, there's no cure you know.

CASEY. No?

GLADYS. No. You just keep on twitching and then you die.

CASEY. Twitching?

GLADYS. Yes, look at him.

(**BEN** *is still trying to get free*)

CASEY. Why don't you freshen up a little and then I'll show you the rest of the house.

GLADYS. We'll be right out as soon as Fred does the unpacking, won't we Fred? (*Exit bedroom 2.*)

FRED. (*Following her*) Yes dear. (*Closes the door*)

CASEY. (*Turns D.S. and mouths the words "yes dear."*) Ben, for heaven's sakes, stop fooling around and get Cott to check the air pressure in the ion chamber. They're going to want to use it in a few minutes. I'm going to check the bathroom. (*Exit bathroom*)

BEN. Casey –

(*But she has gone.* **BEN** *wriggles and contorts again, then has a brilliant idea. He undoes his belt and zipper and wriggles out of his pants, which remain firmly attached to the cylinder. He stands up for a moment in his boxer shorts then, with a "whoosh," his pants disappear down the cylinder. Enter* **SUE** *from the kitchen,* **BEN** *starts to move below the counter to hide, but as he moves closer to the cylinder he is instantly sucked onto it again. He sits there, trying to look nonchalant as* **SUE** *comes L.*)

SUE. Hello. (*She pauses and looks at him*) You know, I don't think I'm going to ask what it is you're doing.

BEN. Please, this thing is lethal. Switch it off for me will you.

SUE. (*Gets the remote*) What number switches if off?

BEN. Oh Lord, I don't know. Try twenty-seven again.

SUE. O.K. Here goes.

(*She clicks the remote and* **BEN** *stands up,* **SUE** *giggles*)

BEN. Thank you. (*He sees her laughing, looks down at his boxers and moves quickly L. to the couch and grabs a cushion, which he holds in front of himself.*) What are you laughing at?

SUE. Your legs.

BEN. What's wrong with my legs?

SUE. (*Still laughing*) Oh, nothing I suppose, as long as you're living on the planet of the chickens.

BEN. That's not fair.

SUE. I'm sorry, but if you don't mind my asking, why have you taken your pants off?

BEN. I haven't taken them off, well, I have – what I mean is that infernal trash machine swallowed them.

SUE. (*Looks down the trash cylinder*) I don't see them, they've disappeared.

(**BEN** *comes R. and bends down to look*)

CASEY. (*Enters from the bathroom*) Now that's not a pretty sight!

(**BEN** *moves quickly below the kitchen counter so* **CASEY** *can't see him and holds the cushion in front of him*)

Have you got Cott to check the ion chamber?

BEN. Well, no, you see I never got the chance –

CASEY. Oh Ben, you're hopeless. Never mind, I'll get him. (*Exit R. to the kitchen.*)

BEN. What am I going to wear?

SUE. You don't have any other pants here?

BEN. No. We were only supposed to be here for one day.

GLADYS. (*Enters from bedroom 2. Her mouth never stops.*) Now make sure all my things are in the top two drawers. You know I don't like to bend down, then find out where the telephones are and be sure to put all your things away, and don't just throw them in the drawer, I want everything neat and tidy when I get back, and keep studying all those numbers for the remote. As soon as I've finished in the bathroom, we're going to try that ion chamber. (*Exit to bathroom and closes the door*)

FRED. (*Off*) Yes dear.

SUE. Why does he put up with that?

BEN. It's hard to figure, isn't it.

SUE. Ah well, I'd better get on with dinner. (*Exit R. to the kitchen*)

BEN. What am I going to wear? (*But she has gone*) Oh Lord, I can't walk around holding a cushion all night.

(*Enter* COTT *and* CASEY *from the kitchen.* BEN *stays below the counter, holding the cushion.* COTT *goes in the ion chamber.*)

CASEY. (*Comes L. and D. a little and looks at* BEN) I've seen better shaped legs on a table.

BEN. There's nothing wrong with my legs.

CASEY. (*Giggles*)

BEN. What's so funny?

CASEY. (*Still giggling*) If we get you an eye-patch, you could be "Rooster Cogburn."

BEN. Very funny.

CASEY. Ben, where are your pants?

BEN. The trash disposal got them.

CASEY. Why did you take them off?

BEN. (*Still below the counter*) Well I didn't – oh never mind, what am I going to wear?

COTT. (*Re-appears from the chamber.*) I've checked the pressure at the top, it should be O.K. now.

CASEY. Alright, but let's test it before Godzilla gets back here.

COTT. O.K., get in.

CASEY. Why me, why not you?

COTT. Me? You know I might if I could lie down. It might be good for my rheumatism, but standing up? You've got to be kidding. I've got this irregular heartbeat, an embolism, chronic colitis and two double hernias.

BEN. (*Teasing*) Are you sure there's nothing else wrong with you?

CASEY. I don't think we should go down that road.

COTT. As a matter of fact, –

CASEY. Down the road we go!

COTT. (*Looks briefly at her and doesn't miss a beat*) – just for your information young man, I happen to be in a very delicate condition because of a hereditary arterial blockage, which affects my inner ear and any sudden movement could trigger uncontrollable convulsions starting in my legs and spreading rapidly to the rest of my body. I'm not going in that contraption.

CASEY. Well, what about you Ben?

BEN. Oh no. Not me. I've already done it once.

CASEY. Alright then, I'll do it.

   (*She gets in.* **COTT** *closes the door*)

COTT. You got a remote Ben?

BEN. Yeah. Right here on the counter.

COTT. O.K. Press thirty-three.

BEN. O.K. (*Clicks the remote*)

   (*There is a bloodcurdling yell from* **CASEY** *in the chamber.*)

COTT. Open it quick.

BEN.O.K.

   (*He fiddles for a moment then clicks the remote. The door opens and we see* **CASEY**, *her hair is straight up in the air* (*SEE AUTHOR'S NOTES.*) *and her skirt around her neck. The door closes and there is another yell from* **CASEY**.)

COTT. Get her out of there.

   (**BEN** *clicks the remote and the door opens.*)

CASEY. (*Her hair back to normal, staggers out pulling down her skirt.*) That thing is lethal.

BEN. I'm sorry, I guess I kept my finger on the button too long.

COTT. That's probably it. Just a touch does it. It's a very delicate mechanism, but it's got too much pressure at the top. I've got to bleed the system, it won't take a minute.

   (*He steps into the chamber, takes a screwdriver out of his tool belt and fiddles above his head.*)

CASEY. (*Looking at* BEN *still holding the cushion*) Look Ben, you can't walk around here wearing a cushion all night. How in heavens name did you manage to put your pants down the trash disposal.

BEN. I didn't put them down there, they just sort of got sucked in, it swallowed them.

(CASEY *laughs and opens her mouth to say something*)

And I don't want to hear any more chicken jokes. Mr. Cott, where do things go when they get sucked down that trash disposal?

COTT. (*Puts his head out of the chamber.*) They go to this giant grinder in the control room.

BEN. Oh Lord. You don't have a spare pair of pants do you?

COTT. Not me. (*Returns to the chamber.*)

BEN. What am I going to do?

CASEY. Well, you could flap your wings and run around the room.

BEN. That's not funny.

GLADYS. (*Enters from the bathroom.*) You there! Have you finished cleaning that ion thing?

CASEY. (*Softly*) Mr. Cott, have I finished cleaning the ion thing?

GLADYS. I heard that. Who's Mr. Cott?

CASEY. He's er – er – there is no Mr. Cott.

GLADYS. I distinctly heard you say Mr. Cott.

CASEY. No – No. I said, er- er- Miss Turcotte. Yes, that's it, Miss Turcotte.

GLADYS. Miss Turcotte? Who's she? What's she doing here?

CASEY. Er – er – she's the children's nanny. Yes that's it, she's the nanny.

GLADYS. I'll be out in a few minutes to meet her. (*She goes into bedroom 2, closing the door.*) Fred, haven't you finished unpacking yet?

BEN. Why did you tell her there's a nanny here?

CASEY. You heard her. We can't let her know Cott is the maintenance man.

BEN. She just said she was coming out to meet Miss Turcotte.

CASEY. And so she will. Ben, can you get Sue in here please.

(**BEN** *exits R. in the kitchen*)

Mr. Cott, have you finished?

COTT. (*Comes out of the chamber.*) Yeah, It should be O.K. now.

CASEY. Listen, Mrs. McNicoll just heard me call you Mister Cott.

COTT. That's torn it.

CASEY. We can still salvage this. I just told her you weren't Mister Cott, but Miss Turcotte, the children's nanny.

COTT. Why on earth would you do that.?

(**CASEY** *just looks at him*)

Oh no! I draw the line at that.

CASEY. For five thousand dollars you can do it.

COTT. What would I wear?

(*Enter* **SUE** *and* **BEN** *from the kitchen.*)

CASEY. I thought so. That's a wrap-around skirt isn't it?

SUE. Well, yes.

CASEY. Do you suppose Mr. Cott could borrow it?

(*There's a pause*)

SUE. You know, I don't want to appear overly curious or presumptuous, but what in the world does Mr. Cott want with my skirt?

CASEY. He wants to wear it.

BEN. This I've got to see.

COTT. There's no way I'm wearing a skirt.

CASEY. Ah well, it was nice while it lasted, but good-bye five thousand dollars.

COTT/BEN. (*Together*) What?

CASEY. If the dragon lady finds out Mr. Cott is the maintenance man, it's probably all over.

COTT. I need that five thousand dollars.

BEN. So do I.

CASEY. And so do I.

(BEN *and* CASEY *look at* COTT.)

COTT. Alright, I'll do it.

SUE. Aren't you all forgetting something?

CASEY. What?

SUE. It's my skirt and I have absolutely no intention of taking it off.

CASEY. I see.

SUE. But, I could be persuaded.

CASEY. How?

SUE. You all get five thousand dollars if the house sells, right?

CASEY. Yes.

SUE. Not any more. You each have to pay me one thousand dollars.

COTT. Now wait a minute.

CASEY. It's our only chance.

COTT. What about you Ben?

BEN. Well, four thousand is better than nothing.

CASEY. I agree

COTT. Oh, alright then.

SUE. O.K. Mr. Cott, you come with me. Let's see what you look like in a skirt.

BEN. What about his hair?

CASEY. That's a good point, I know, I've got a shower cap and some rollers in my bag. Hold on a second, I'll be right back. (*Exits in a hurry U.L.*)

COTT. Hair rollers! I don't think so.

BEN. Come on Mr. Cott. I need the money.

SUE. So do I. Please.

COTT. You know, none of this is really getting us anywhere.

BEN. We're not going anywhere.

CASEY. (*Enters from U.L. with a plastic bag.*) Here take these.

SUE. (*Takes the bag.*) O.K. What about, you know, (*She cups her hands to indicate them*) boobs?

CASEY. (*Grabs a couple of balloons off the wall*) Here, use these.

SUE. Right, leave it to me. Come on Mr. Cott, let's see what we can do with you.

CASEY. How's the ion chamber?

COTT. It should be O.K. now.

(**COTT** *and* **SUE** *exit R. to the kitchen*)

CASEY. O.K. So far, so good.

BEN. You may not have noticed, but I still have no pants, and now Sue won't have a skirt. This place is going to look like a strip joint.

CASEY. Why don't you wear Cott's pants?

BEN. No one is going to believe this.

CASEY. Go!

(*Enter* **GLADYS** *from bedroom 2, followed by* **FRED**. **BEN** *quickly retreats below the counter.*)

GLADYS. Is the chamber ready?

CASEY. Yes Ma'am, it's all clean.

GLADYS. Good. Fred, you get in.

FRED. Me?

GLADYS. Yes, I don't trust it.

(**FRED** *gets in and closes the door*)

(*They all stand and watch.*)

GLADYS. How do you know if it's working?

CASEY. Have you pressed the remote?

GLADYS. (*Yells at the chamber door*) Fred, press the remote. What's that? How do I know what number to press.

You've got the remote and anyway I told you to memorize the numbers.

CASEY. (*Looking at her brochure.*)) It's number thirty-three.

GLADYS. (*Yells at the chamber door.*) It's thirty-three Fred.

BEN. Casey, are you sure-

GLADYS. I heard that. Are you sure what?

BEN. I was going to say – (*He stops, pauses and looks around*)-
wait a minute, am I going to get a fair hearing on this?

CASEY. I'm sure Ben was just concerned that the chamber
was clean enough, isn't that right Ben?

BEN. Well actually, I was – er – (**CASEY** *glares at him.*) yes
that's right.

FRED. (*The chamber door opens and he steps out*) That's rather
fun.

CASEY. You're alright?

FRED. Of course.

GLADYS. Are you still in one piece Fred?

FRED. Of course dear. I feel wonderful.

BEN. It actually worked.

FRED. Like a charm. I got this warm fuzzy feeling. Very
mild though. How do you boost it up a bit?

CASEY. I don't think we want to do that.

GLADYS. Warm fuzzy feeling? I don't like the sound of that.
I don't want you going in there again Fred, it might
set you off.

FRED. Why don't you try it dear?

GLADYS. Are you telling me what to do again?

FRED. Oh no dear.

GLADYS. Good. I know, why don't I try it. (*She gets in and
closes the door.*)

CASEY. You'll have to press thirty-three again.

FRED. I know, but it's so nice and quiet. I thought I'd just
wait a minute.

GLADYS. (*Off*) Fred, press the number.

FRED. I will in just a minute dear. (*He grins at* **BEN** *and*
CASEY)

BEN. How long have you been married?

FRED. Since 1897.

GLADYS. (*Off*) Fred, what are you waiting for? Get it started.

FRED. Ah well, peace and quiet can't last for ever. (*He clicks the remote.*)

(*Enter* **SUE** *from the kitchen. She's now wearing a large chef's apron with a bib-top, tied at the waist, and reaching almost to her feet. We will see in a moment or two, when we see her from behind, that she is now minus her skirt.*)

SUE. Oh, hi! How was the room?

FRED. Just fine thanks.

(*Muffled noises off from* **GLADYS**)

SUE. Is she always like that?

FRED. Like what?

SUE. Well, you know –

FRED. It's probably the phase of the moon.

SUE. What phase?

FRED. Whatever phase it's in.

(*The chamber door opens and* **GLADYS** *steps out*).

GLADYS. What were you doing Fred? You left me standing there.

CASEY. Are you alright Mrs. McNicoll?

GLADYS. Of course I'm alright. Why wouldn't I be alright?

FRED. How do you feel dear?

GLADYS. Well I most certainly don't have a warm fuzzy feeling, if that's what you mean, so you can take that big silly grin off your face. Now where's that Nanny?

CASEY. She's – er changing, she'll be in, in a few minutes.

(**BEN**, *below the counter has been signaling to* **SUE** *to come and help him hide the fact that he is not wearing any pants.* **GLADYS** *sees this.*)

GLADYS. Ah! Twitching again. Oh well, I suppose you can't help it.

BEN. Twitching?

CASEY. Yes, you twitch because you have this fatal disease.

BEN. I do?

CASEY. Yes. (*Whispers*) So twitch! (**BEN** *signals to* **SUE** *again*)

GLADYS. Right Fred, come and sit down and you can tell me everything you've found out about this house.

(**FRED** *and* **GLADYS** *move L. to sit on the couch.* **BEN** *tries to hide behind a stool and signals to* **SUE** *again.* **GLADYS** *sees him.*)

Do you suppose you could go and twitch somewhere else?

BEN. Right! Yes!

(*He signals to* **SUE** *again who finally gets the message and comes D.R. below the counter taking care that her derriere is never facing* **GLADYS** *and* **FRED**.)

I'll go and help Sue in the kitchen.

(**SUE** *comes D.R. and stands immediately to* **BEN**'s *left. She unties her apron from the waist. We see that she's now minus her skirt because we catch just a glimpse of lacy undies.* **BEN** *snuggles up close behind her and holds the sides of her apron around him. They move together, taking little shuffle steps, always facing* **GLADYS** *and* **FRED**.)

GLADYS. What are you doing?

CASEY. Well – er – you see. If he holds onto someone, it helps him to stop twitching.

GLADYS. I asked him, not you. (*Pauses*) Well?

BEN. Well, you see I'm learning to cook from Sue the chef, but I always seem to be one step behind.

GLADYS. Behind what?

BEN. Well – er – you know – (*Looks down at* **SUE**) behind the behind.

GLADYS. Behind what behind? Oooh! Fred, does that mean what I think it means?

FRED. What do you think it means?

GLADYS. I'll ask the questions Fred, if you don't mind.

(**SUE/BEN** *move backwards U.S. maneuvering to exit R. in the kitchen. One of Ben's hands is inside the apron.* **GLADYS** *turns to* **CASEY**.)

Your husband is very familiar with the chef. Don't you think so Fred?

FRED. I guess it's alright.

GLADYS. It most certainly is not, and why are you always standing right behind her?

BEN. Well, as I said, I'm learning to cook and I'm trying to keep in touch.

GLADYS. That's disgusting.

BEN. In any event it's important for me to keep my hand in – I mean out. (*He pulls his hand out*)

(**GLADYS** *gets up and goes R. to take a close look at* **SUE/BEN**. **SUE** *remains facing* **GLADYS** *directly at all times. She gets upstage of them a little so they have to turn and Ben's boxers become visible to the audience, but not to* **FRED**.)

GLADYS. Maybe you're right, he does seem to have stopped twitching. Now, what time is dinner?

SUE. Will about half an hour be O.K.?

GLADYS. That'll be fine. Fred doesn't like to eat too late, do you Fred?

FRED. No dear.

SUE. Right, I'll go and get on with it then.

BEN. Can I help?

SUE. Sure, come on Ben, I'll give you your first cooking lesson. (*They shuffle backwards and exit R. to the kitchen.*)

CASEY. Me too. (*Exit R. in the kitchen.*)

GLADYS. Now Fred, where are all these telephones you were telling me about?

FRED. Well dear, they're all over the place. That vase on the mantle is one of them.

GLADYS. (*Goes R. to the fireplace*) How does it work?

FRED. (*Looking at his brochure*) It says you just twist it to the right.

GLADYS. (*Turns the vase*) Nothing happened.

FRED. Are you sure?

GLADYS. Of course I'm sure. What sort of question is that?

FRED. (*Still reading the brochure*) Apparently it's voice activated. Can you hear a dial tone?

GLADYS. Unfortunately no.

(*Four phones ring simultaneously,* **CASEY** *rushes in from the kitchen*)

CASEY. What happened?

GLADYS. Suddenly every phone in the house started ringing.

CASEY. You must have said their numbers.

GLADYS. I did no such thing! How do you stop them?

FRED. Just turn it back to the left dear. (*She does and the ringing stops*) I'm afraid you did say the numbers, that's what made them ring.

GLADYS. Are you arguing with me Fred?

FRED. You said, unfortunately. Don't you see? One-Four-Two and Eight-ly, and numbers one, four, two and eight all rang.

GLADYS. (*For the first time really deflated and speechless*) Oh!

FRED. You're welcome.

GLADYS. What?

FRED. Oh nothing dear, for a moment I thought you apologized.

GLADYS. What?

CASEY. Well, if everything is O.K., I'll get back to the kitchen. (*Exit R.*)

FRED. (*Reading from the brochure*) This is interesting, it says that that is a self-lighting fireplace. It's number seventeen. Shall I try it?

GLADYS. (*Bends down to look and puts her head into the fireplace*) Alright.

(**FRED** *clicks the remote and the fireplace does its usual bang routine.* **GLADYS** *leaps backwards, her face covered with soot.*)

Oh – oh – oh!

FRED. (*Goes D.L. to help her*) Are you alright dear?

GLADYS. Do I look as though I'm alright.

FRED. I guess you shouldn't have had your head in the fireplace.

GLADYS. Don't tell me what I should and shouldn't do. I need a drink of water.

FRED. I'll get it for you dear.

(*Goes up to the kitchen, opens a cupboard and takes out a glass, as* **GLADYS** *follows him and stands by the fridge, he takes a pitcher of water out of the fridge, closes the door and pours.*)

Why don't you use the bathroom of the future and clean up dear?

GLADYS. Are you telling me what to do again?

FRED. No dear.

GLADYS. Good. I'll tell you what, why don't I go and clean up?

(*The front door bell rings. The fridge door opens and hits* **GLADYS** *in the rear.*)

GLADYS. Oh – Oh – Oh! (*She staggers L. and exits to the bathroom, as* **FRED** *follows her L. a little.*)

(*The door chimes continue as* **CASEY** *comes running out of the kitchen. She closes the fridge door and the chimes stop.*)

FRED. (*Looking at his brochure.*) It says here there's an automatic laundry transporter in the master bedroom, would you mind if I check it out?

CASEY. Not at all, first room on the right down the hall.

FRED. Thanks. (*Exits L.*)

CASEY. (*Rushes D.R. and opens the front door. The fireplace does its bang routine.*) Come in, come in.

(*We see it's still snowing.* **CASEY** *closes the door as* **MR. BROOKS** *steps into the room. He is wearing a hat, a scarf and a heavy overcoat over a conservative business suit. He is perhaps 55 or 60 and when we first meet him he seems a nice enough guy, but as we shall see, he turns into a lecher of gigantic proportions.*)

BROOKS. Casey, good heavens, it's you.

CASEY. Mr. Brooks! What are you doing here?

BROOKS. Is that the sort of welcome you give to your future father-in-law?

CASEY. I'm sorry. Let me take your coat. But what are you doing here?

BROOKS. (*Takes off his hat, scarf and coat.*) I was on my way home and my car got stuck in a snowdrift just down the road.

CASEY. I see.

BROOKS. David said you had to work tonight, what are you doing here?

CASEY. This is where Mr. Broadbent has us working tonight, in this house.

BROOKS. Why?

CASEY. We're trying to sell it.

BROOKS. Oh, I see.

CASEY. You look pretty cold. You want a drink or something? I think there's some wine somewhere.

BROOKS. That would be good. Thanks.

CASEY. Grab a seat, I'll see what I can find.

BROOKS. (*Sits on the R. stool and dumps his hat coat and scarf on the L. one*) You're not a sales person, how come he's got you working on selling this house?

CASEY. (*Gets a bottle of wine out of the fridge*) Well, it's a long story but...

Enter **BEN** *from R. in the kitchen. He is now wearing Cott's blue jeans* (*SEE AUTHOR'S NOTES.*)

BEN. Oh, hi!

BROOKS. Hello

BEN. I'm Ben Adams.

BROOKS. I'm Walter Brooks, my car just got stuck in a snowdrift.

CASEY. Ben, Mr. Brooks is David's dad. You remember my fiancé, David.

BEN. Oh sure.

BROOKS. Are you buying or selling the house?

BEN. Oh I'm with Casey and we're selling it hopefully to a Mr. and Mrs. McNicoll. By the way Casey, where are they?

CASEY. I'm not sure where Godzilla is, but he's in the master bedroom.

BEN. What's he doing in our bedroom?

BROOKS. Our bedroom?

CASEY. Ah, well, er – when he said our bedroom, he didn't mean ours, as in his and mine, he meant ours, as in his and his wife's.

BEN. That makes a lot of sense.

CASEY. The bedroom of him and his wife – Sue, yes, that's it. (*Glaring at* **BEN**) his wife, Sue.

BEN. Who?

CASEY. (*Softly to* **BEN**) This is my fiancé's father, so Sue is your wife, O.K? (*She is pouring a glass of wine*)

BEN. I guess.

BROOKS. You still haven't told me what you're doing here.

CASEY. Well, er – I'm the cook. Mr. Broadbent thought it would be a good idea if we cooked a birthday dinner for Mr. and Mrs. McNicoll.

BROOKS. I didn't know anyone cooked these days. I thought it was something you just watched on television.

CASEY. O.K., here's your drink (*Pushes the glass of wine across the counter*) and then you can be on your way.

BROOKS. That's absolutely out of the question.

CASEY. What?

BROOKS. It's blowing a gale out there. There were two and three foot snowdrifts. Nobody is going anywhere tonight.

CASEY. Oh dear, this really complicates things. Why don't you sit on the couch and finish your drink while Ben and I go and talk to Sue.

(*Enter* **SUE**, *still in her apron and minus her skirt. She's pushing a reluctant* **COTT** *ahead of her. They move L. in front of the ion chamber He is now NANNY! His hair is done up in large " hotpink" rollers. He is wearing a blouse, hastily converted from his work shirt, which has been cut to allow the lower portion to tie in a bow at the front. He has absolutely enormous bosoms! Sue's skirt and his own big leather work boots and red socks complete the picture, which is one of a "very ugly looking broad!"*)

COTT. (*To Casey*) Before you say anything – don't say anything.

CASEY. Sh!

COTT. No one's going to believe I'm a nanny.

CASEY. (*Indicates* **BROOKS**.) Sh!

BROOKS. (*Stands*) Aren't you going to introduce us?

CASEY. Yes, of course. Mr. Brooks, this is Miss Turcotte.

BEN. She's the nanny.

COTT. (*Goes D.R. to shake hands with* **BROOKS**) (*In a high voice*) Yes, that's me, Nanny Turcotte.

BROOKS. How do you do?

COTT. Hello.

BROOKS. So, how old are the children?

(*Everybody looks at each other*)

CASEY. (*Together*) Nine.

BEN. Six.

(*Pause*)

CASEY. (*Together*) Six

BEN. Nine

CASEY. Well, Jennifer is nine and little Luke is six.

BROOKS. (*To* SUE) And you must be Mrs. Adams.

SUE. Me?

BROOKS. You don't look old enough to have a nine year old.

SUE. What, me?

CASEY. Yes, well, we'll talk about that later shall we?

SUE. What's going on?

CASEY. We need to talk in the kitchen. We'll leave Mr. Brooks and Nanny to get acquainted while we talk. (*She almost drags* SUE *off towards the kitchen*)

BEN. (*Following* CASEY *and* SUE) You know Casey, for someone who's only recently taken up lying, you're showing a real flair for it.

(**CASEY** *glares back at* **BEN** *before they enter the kitchen.*)

BROOKS. Why don't you sit down Nanny.

COTT. Oh, alright. (*Sits next to* **BROOKS** *on the couch.*)

BROOKS. My, my, you are a big girl aren't you?

COTT. Now, now Mr. Brooks, let's not get personal.

BROOKS. I didn't mean to be personal, it's just that, well, I find you very attractive.

COTT. Me?

BROOKS. Oh yes.

COTT. Oh no.

BROOKS. Oh yes.

COTT. Oh dear!

BROOKS. Why don't you call me Walter. You see, I've been divorced for a number of years, but when I saw you, I felt this stirring inside me.

COTT. Stirring?

BROOKS. Oh yes! (*He slowly puts his hand on Cott's knee*)

COTT. (*Leaps up and backs away R.*) Mr. Brooks, you naughty boy. Just keep your hands to yourself. I'm not that sort of girl.

BROOKS. (*Gets up and follows him R.*) And just what sort of girl are you Nanny?

COTT. You'd be surprised.

BROOKS. Oh, I like surprises.

COTT. You wouldn't like this one.

BROOKS. (*Still advancing*) I've always had this thing for Nannies.

COTT. Yes, well, this Nanny doesn't have a thing for you.

BROOKS. Come now Nanny, there's romance and excitement in the air, can't you feel it?

COTT. (*Still backing away, reaches the counter and escapes D.R.*) No, and you're not going to feel it either.

BROOKS. (*Stops the chase, returns to the couch and sits, L. side.*) I'm sorry. I don't know what got into me. I'm afraid I just got a little carried away.

COTT. That's better. Now for heaven's sake, calm down, will you.

BROOKS. It's just that there is something about you that absolutely fascinates me.

COTT. I'm sure you're going to tell me it's my vibrant personality. (*Follows him R. and sits on the couch, R. side.*)

BROOKS. No, actually it's not. I don't want to burst your balloon, but –

COTT. You'd better not get anywhere near my balloons.

BROOKS. It's your feet!

COTT. What?

BROOKS. Your big, beautiful feet.

COTT. You're nuts, you know that don't you?

BROOKS. Yes, nuts about you Nanny.

COTT. Let's change the subject from nuts shall we.

(**BROOKS** *tries to grab* **COTT,** *who puts up a knee, which catches* **BROOKS** *in the groin. He collapses on the floor with a groan, holding his crotch.*)

BROOKS. Ooh – Ooh – Ooh – I'm going to die.

(*The noise brings* **CASEY**, **BEN** *and* **SUE** *out of the kitchen.*)

BEN. What happened?

BROOKS. Ooh – ooh – ooh!

SUE. Why don't you sit down?

BROOKS. I don't think sitting would be very good right now. Could I lie down somewhere?

CASEY. You'd better take this other bedroom. (*She indicates B.R.1*)

BROOKS. Thank you. (*Exits to B.R.1 and closes the door.*)

COTT. Now look here you guys, this Nanny thing has gone far enough. I've got problems. You guys don't seem to realize what's going on. My blood pressure is rising, I can feel it you know, and what with my history of congenital angina along with a recurrence of my kidney stones, coupled with a blockage in my aorta, I could be gone any moment.

CASEY. If you could just hold that thought for a moment, there's a couple of things we need to straighten out.

SUE. What things?

CASEY. Oh, just a couple of minor details.

SUE. Such as?

BEN. This I've got to hear.

SUE. What are you all talking about?

BEN. Let me refresh your memory about these "minor details." First: Mr. and Mrs. McNicoll think Casey and I are married and you are the cook. Second: Mr. Brooks thinks you and I are married and Casey is the cook. You have no skirt, I've lost my pants, we're all stuck here for the whole night and Casey and I now have to share the master bedroom.

SUE. I don't understand.

CASEY. Well, Mr. Brooks is my fiancé's Dad. I couldn't tell him I was Ben's wife now, could I?

SUE. It might have been better than the mess we're in now.

COTT. You think you're in a mess. Wait till I tell you about Mr. "I can't keep my hands to myself," Casanova Brooks.

CASEY. Shhh!

FRED. (*Enters from U.L.*) Oh. Hi you guys. (*Opens the door and looks in B.R.2.*) Is Mrs. McNicoll still in the bathroom?

CASEY. I guess so, we haven't seen her.

FRED. Good. So peace and quiet reign for a while.

GLADYS. (*Her face now clean, comes out of the bathroom.*) I heard that Fred. There was definitely innuendo in that remark. I'm going to put on a new face, and then we'll get ready for dinner. Put some fresh towels out for me. I'll be back in a minute. (*Exits to bedroom 2.*)

FRED. Yes my little piranha fish. (*Exits to the bathroom and closes the door.*)

CASEY. Now, where were we?

COTT. We were talking about Mr. "Reach out and touch someone" Brooks.

BEN. So what are we going to do?

SUE. What's all this about me being Ben's wife?

BEN. How can I be married to two people?

CASEY. I think we can still pull it off.

BEN. For heaven's sake how? We're all in the same house.

CASEY. O.K., first we make sure that Sue and I are never together when Godzilla and Pussy-cat and Mr. Brooks are in the same room, then we just refer to Ben's wife and the chef without ever saying who is who.

SUE. You think that'll work?

CASEY. Just make sure you and Ben act like you're married when Mr. Brooks is around and Ben and I will act like we're married when Mr. and Mrs. McNicoll are there.

SUE. (*Snuggles up to* **BEN.**) So, I get to be Mrs. Adams.

BEN. None of this is going to work.

SUE. Come on Ben. This will be fun. (*She reaches to put her arms round him and accidentally hits the automatic cleaning switch for the bathroom. The red light above the bathroom door starts flashing.*) OOPS!

CASEY. Isn't Fred in there?

SUE. Can you stop it?

COTT. Once it's started you can't switch it off. I'll have to take the switch plate off the wall and disconnect it. I'll need a screwdriver. (*He hurries off R.*)

(**CASEY, BEN** *and* **SUE** *are all just to the L of the bathroom door facing U.S., looking anxiously at it. During the following conversation,* **BROOKS**, *unseen by them, creeps furtively out of B.R. 1 and exits R. into the kitchen.*)

BEN. I'm telling you none of this is going to work.

CASEY. Of course it is, it's really very simple.

BEN. You think so? It wasn't simple when I just had to be married to Casey, now I've got two wives, two children and a Nanny. One of my wives has a fiancé whose father is here, Godzilla looks like Queen Kong, Pussycat is about to drown, Cott says he's about to die and and all you can say is "it's really very simple." Oh, and did I mention that lover boy Brooks seems to be a sexmaniac who has taken a fancy to Nanny Turcotte.

SUE. You know I nearly got a job as a nanny once.

BEN. What happened?

SUE. Well, I was going for the interview, but –

SUE. BEN/CASEY. (*Join in*) I got on the wrong bus and ended up in Milwaukee.

(**COTT** *runs out of the kitchen,* **BROOKS** *is right behind him, arms outstretched trying to grab him.* **COTT** *looks desperately around for a way to escape, sees the front door and runs to it followed by* **BROOKS**. *When he gets there he opens the door, steps quickly to one side and* **BROOKS** *runs straight through it, aided by a swift kick in the pants from* **COTT** *who closes the door and locks it. A buzzer sounds, the red light stops flashing and* **FRED**, *soaking wet from head to foot, staggers out of the bathroom as the curtain falls.*)

ACT II

LATER THE SAME EVENING

(*Enter* **CASEY** *from the kitchen. She is dressed as before, and carrying a tray with cups, saucers, and a coffee pot. She is followed by* **BEN.** *He is wearing the large apron and no pants, his boxer shorts very visible from the rear. He has removed his jacket and we now see he has on a short-sleeved shirt. He carries a tray with a large cake on it, small plates and desert forks. The cake should have lots of very soft frosting.*)

CASEY. (*Crosses L. to the coffee table and starts arranging coffee cups etc.*) I must say dinner went rather well, don't you think.

BEN. (*Follows her L. and puts his tray down*) How the dragon lady hasn't figured out what's going on beats me.

CASEY. I must admit there were one or two difficult moments, but it seemed to work. Sue and I kept alternating in the kitchen, and you never referred to anyone by name, just kept talking about your wife and the cook, so they never knew who was who.

BEN. It's all going to go wrong you know.

CASEY. Think positively Ben, we're O.K. so far. Even Fred didn't seem too upset about getting locked in the bathroom.

BEN. How does he stand that woman?

CASEY. Who knows?

BEN. Compared to her, a great white shark is warm and cuddly.

CASEY. (*Laughs*) Oh Ben!

BEN. Well, no one seems to be thinking of me. I had to give Fred Cott's jeans, so here I am with no pants again.

CASEY. You look O.K. from the front so try to hang on till we get Fred's clothes out of the dryer. Remember now, if there's an awkward moment, or a question you don't want to answer, just start twitching.

(*Enter* **COTT** *from R. in the kitchen. He is still Nanny, but has his air cylinder*).

COTT. (*To himself as he goes D.R. to the closet, clicks his remote, the closet opens and he leans in to top off the air system.*) I'm going to fix that son of a B. If he comes near me once again, I'll be ready. He's going to regret the day he was born. He's going to learn what happens when you mess with Ed Cott, he's going to find out what pain really is, he's going to discover excruciating agony, prolonged indefinitely, he's – – –

CASEY. Please Mr. Cott, it's going so well, let's just try to keep the peace shall we?

COTT. Peace! That's right. I'm going to have a piece of that Brooks character, that's what I'm going to do. (*He has finished topping off the closet, so he sends it back and moves up to the ion chamber. He opens the door, then reaches up and in with his air cylinder.*)

BEN. By the way where is he?

COTT. If you'd let me have my way, I'd have left him outside.

BEN. He'd freeze to death out there. We had to let him back in.

COTT. He's in his room.

CASEY. Are you sure you should be topping that off? It always seems to be too strong or something when you do that.

COTT. (*Ignores her and continues his diatribe*) Oh, it's going to be strong alright, and I'm going to get lover-boy Brooks in it, and he's going to shoot right out of his shorts till he can't tell his elbow from his –

CASEY. Mr. Cott! Why don't you let me take care of him? You're going to spoil our chances at the bonus money.

COTT. Alright, but if he puts his hands anywhere near me again, I'm going to let him have it. (**CASEY** *gives him a "look"*) Alright, alright, I'll be lying down in the control room. I've got three slipped discs you know, I need to get my feet up. (*Exit R. to the kitchen.*)

BEN. I don't believe Brooks. You know, you can hardly blame Cott.

CASEY. I know. I find it hard to believe my fiancé's dad is a sex maniac. Let's just try to keep them apart.

(*Enter **SUE** from the kitchen. She is still minus her skirt and now wears a very short bartender type apron, which just covers her front, but reveals lacy underwear in the rear. She has removed her bulky sweater and is wearing a short sleeve top.*)

SUE. Listen you guys, they're on their way. I'm going to need the big apron back.

BEN. What am I going to wear?

SUE. I don't know, but I can't keep going like this. They're beginning to think something's wrong. I had to walk out of the dining room backwards. I mean look at me.

(*She turns to **CASEY** and the audience can see her undies from the rear*)

CASEY. Well, maybe we could accessorize it a bit.

SUE. With what? A lamp post and a public defender? (*She looks off R.*) Oh Lord! Here they come. Ben, help me.

(***BEN** swings her around and into the open doorway of the ion chamber and almost closes the door. **SUE**, now right behind **BEN**, puts her arms around his waist. He takes the arms away and pushes them behind him. They return, he pushes them behind him again. Her right arm returns just as **GLADYS** and **FRED**, now wearing Cott's jeans, enter from the kitchen. **BEN** quickly puts his own right arm behind his back, leaving Sue's right arm looking as though it was his. As **FRED** and **GLADYS** cross L. in front of him on their way to the couch, **BEN** tries to grab Sue's hand to remove it. **GLADYS** turns to look,* *but* **BEN** *recovers by replacing his own arm behind him in the nick of time.* **GLADYS** *frowns and looks at him, so* **BEN** *starts twitching. During the following conversation, Sue's hand and fingers move in little circles all over Ben's chest watched by everybody.* **BEN** *twitches and wriggles uncomfortably as the hand moves lower and lower, perilously close to forbidden territory.* **BEN** *moves it higher with his left hand, but it starts its downward trek again. The sequence is repeated several times.*)

GLADYS. (*Crosses L. to the couch and starts cutting the cake*) I must say, that was an excellent meal. Don't you think so Fred? (**FRED** *opens his mouth to say something, but* **GLADYS** *presses right on*) Fred gives his compliments to the chef. Don't you Fred? I'm beginning to get quite a favorable impression of this house.

CASEY. I'm so glad you like it.

GLADYS. Fred likes it too, don't you Fred?

FRED. Well, there was this bathroom thing.

GLADYS. (*Ignores* **FRED** *and looks over at* **BEN** *who is still trying to deal with Sue's wandering hand.*) Young man, I know you have this terrible affliction, but please try to control yourself.

BEN. Of course madam. (*Over his shoulder to* **SUE**.) There's someone else who should control themselves.

GLADYS. Here you are Fred, (*She hands him a plate*) take Mr. Adams some cake, it might help his twitching.

FRED. Very well dear.

(*He crosses U.R. with a plate, with cake and a fork on it, and hands it to* **BEN** *who takes it in his left hand.*)

BEN. Thank you. (**FRED** *returns to the couch.*)

(*Sue's right hand tries unsuccessfully to find the fork. They all watch as* **SUE** *knocks the fork onto the floor*)

Oh, silly me.

GLADYS. (*Who has been watching all this.*)Young man, I do understand that you do have difficulty with muscular control, so, under the circumstances, I think it would be acceptable for you to eat your cake with your fingers.

BEN. Thank you.

CASEY. (*Trying to divert attention from* **BEN.**) Shall I pour the coffee?

GLADYS. Thank you, but Fred will do it. He always does, don't you Fred?

(**FRED** *pours coffee and they all watch as* **SUE** *grabs the whole piece of cake in her right hand and tries to find Ben's mouth. Eventually, she pushes the whole piece into his face.*)

I think perhaps you had better help your husband clean up.

CASEY. Right, come on darling.

(*She moves U.R. with a remote in her hand. She sees* **FRED** *and* **GLADYS** *watching so she carefully places herself between them and* **BEN** *so he can remove Sue's hand, which he does.*)

Come on Ben.

(*They shuffle backwards off R. into the kitchen.* **SUE** *hiding behind* **BEN,** *and* **CASEY** *helping to make sure* **FRED** *and* **GLADYS** *see neither Sue's nor Ben's rear.*)

GLADYS. Now Fred, you never did finish explaining these phones to me.

FRED. Alright dear. (*He picks up a brochure from the coffee table and consults it*) They're all over the place, but they don't look like phones. Here, (*He indicates the vase on the mantle*) you take this vase, that's number one. I'll take the peppermill on the counter, that's number four.

(*He crosses R. and* **GLADYS** *gets up and stands by the fireplace*)

Now twist the base of the vase and say "four."

(**GLADYS** *just puts her hands on her hips and glares at him*)

Oh, say "four," please.

GLADYS. (*Acknowledges the "please"*) Four.

(*The peppermill rings, so* **FRED** *picks it up and turns it.*)

FRED. Can you hear me dear?

GLADYS. Oh yes. Well, now isn't that clever.

(*Enter* **COTT** *from the kitchen, dressed as before, but minus his air cylinder. He carries a wicked looking pair of bolt cutters, which he puts down on the kitchen counter. He opens the ion chamber door and is just about to hitch up his skirt, when he sees* **FRED** *and* **GLADYS** *looking at him. He moves into the chamber, now barely visible to* **FRED** *and* **GLADYS**, *but very visible to the audience. He hitches up his skirt, and we see he's still wearing his tool belt. He takes out a screw driver, replaces the skirt, then, standing just inside the chamber door, he reaches up inside it to make an adjustment. Enter* **BROOKS** *from bedroom 1. He sees Nanny, and tip-toes lecherously toward "her" He reaches for* **COTT**, *who yells, grabs the offending hand, swings* **BROOKS** *into the chamber and closes the door. He then presses the remote, there is a yell from* **BROOKS**, *a whining noise and a half second later the door opens to reveal a somewhat disheveled* **BROOKS**. **COTT** *is furiously clicking his remote. Immediately, the door closes and a second or two later we see an even more disheveled* **BROOKS**. *This sequence is repeated several times, watched by* **FRED** *and* **GLADYS**. **FRED** *has flipped his phone switch off, but* **GLADYS** *still has the vase in her hand.* **COTT** *is busy clicking his remote and obviously enjoying himself. Eventually, he relents and* **BROOKS** *staggers out and leans on the kitchen counter.*)

GLADYS. Nanny, what are you doing to that poor, unfortunate man?

(*Phones ring everywhere*)

FRED. (*Flips the light switch.*) Hello.

BROOKS. (*Picks up the peppermill*) Hello.

COTT. (*Steps into the chamber and flips the switch, unseen by* **BROOKS** *who is facing downstage.*) Hello.

FRED. Couldn't you use the word "unlucky"?

BROOKS. I feel lucky tonight. Where are you Nanny Turcotte?

GLADYS. What's going on?

FRED. You said, "unfortunate." Your phone line was open, don't you see? One-four-two-n-eight. Again.

GLADYS. Well, who's on the line?

BROOKS. Is that you Nanny?

COTT. (*Almost to himself*) Oh Lord! I'm too old for this.

BROOKS. Oh, but you've still got it.

COTT. Yes, and you still can't have it.

BROOKS. I want you Nanny, you sexy thing.

GLADYS. What did you say?

FRED. (*Jumps in quickly*) Your phone's the next to ring.

GLADYS. What?

FRED. He said your phone's the next to ring.

GLADYS. What are you talking about?

COTT. I'll tell you what we're talking about. We're talking about a sex-maniac who can't control himself, and just because he's wearing pants, he seems to think that gives him license to put his hands where no hands have gone before.

GLADYS. Pants? Fred, what have you been up to?

FRED. Nothing dear.

GLADYS. Nothing? You heard Nanny!

FRED. It wasn't me, it was him, you saw him.

GLADYS. Him who?

FRED. Him, the other guy.

GLADYS. Fred McNicoll, that's the most pathetic excuse I've ever heard. It doesn't take a great feat of imagination –

BROOKS. (*Interrupts*) Feet! Oh yes Nanny, let's talk about feet.

GLADYS. Why in heaven's name would you want to talk about my feet?

FRED. I don't think it's your feet he wants to talk about dear.

GLADYS. Why not? What's wrong with my feet?

FRED. Nothing dear, but –

BROOKS. Come now Nanny. Why don't you use those big, beautiful feet to take a walk on the wild side and come into the kitchen?

COTT. If I use these big, beautiful feet to take a walk on the wild side into the kitchen, I shall go wild and put one of them in a certain place, which for you will make sitting down extremely painful, walking an excruciating, agonizing effort, and any other extra-curricular activity absolutely impossible.

GLADYS. Fred, what does Nanny mean by that?

FRED. Well, I guess –

GLADYS. I don't want you to guess. I can guess. You're supposed to know.

FRED. Why am I supposed to know?

BROOKS. Now Nanny, let's just ignore these other people on the line and concentrate on that extra-curricular activity you mentioned.

COTT. You've got a one-track mind. I give up.

BROOKS. You give up? Good. I'm going to find you Nanny with your big, beautiful feet, and then I'm going to dance my way right into your heart.

COTT. If you get close enough to my big, beautiful feet, one swift kick in the "you know whats" and the only dance you'll be doing will be the Nutcracker.

BROOKS. I'm coming to get you Nanny Turcotte. I've got kisses for you, you naughty nanny. (*He puts down the peppermill and exits R.*)

COTT. (*Flips the switch, comes out of the chamber and closes the door.*) You'll never kiss this naughty nanny. Come to think of it. I think I know what you can kiss! (*Picks up the bolt cutters and exits R. to the kitchen.*)

GLADYS. Are you still there Fred?

FRED. Of course, I'm still here, you can see me can't you?

GLADYS. Don't be so obstreperous Fred. I meant, are you still on the line?

FRED. Shall we hang up now dear?

GLADYS. Very well.

(*They both "hang up" and* **GLADYS** *returns the vase to the mantle*)

CASEY. (*Enters from the kitchen.*) Ah, trying the phones I see.

(**GLADYS** *sits on the sofa, looks at* **FRED** *and pats the seat beside her.* **FRED** *gives a wistful look at* **CASEY** *as he moves D. to sit by* **GLADYS**.)

GLADYS. Yes. They seem a little bit confusing.

CASEY. (*Starts to clear away the cake, plates, etc.*) I'm sure you'll get used to them. They're really very convenient.

GLADYS. I suppose so. Do you think they're a good idea Fred?

FRED. You're asking me?

GLADYS. Why are you in this belligerent mood Fred?

(**BROOKS** *enters from the kitchen on the dead run. He is followed by* **COTT** *clicking the bolt cutters menacingly. He continues off L. followed by* **COTT**.

CASEY. Oh dear. I think I'd better try and rescue poor Mr. Brooks. (*Exits L.*)

GLADYS. Do you know what's going on Fred?

FRED. Well, dear, it looks like Mr. Brooks has er – er – well –

GLADYS. Out with it Fred.

FRED. Well – er – taken a fancy to Nanny.

GLADYS. Don't be ridiculous Fred. How could anyone in their right mind take a fancy to Nanny?

FRED. I know. It does seem a little strange doesn't it.

GLADYS. I need to talk to Mrs. Adams about Mr. Brooks' behavior, and his pursuit of Nanny, so get your mind off that ion chamber, it might set you off again.

(*Enter* **CASEY** *and* **COTT** *from U.L.* **CASEY** *is pushing a reluctant* **COTT**.)

CASEY. There, there, Nanny, we'll just let Mr. Brooks cool down a bit. Why don't you go into the kitchen, and make yourself a nice cup of hot tea.

GLADYS. (*So engrossed in her own thoughts, and almost to her-self.*) I'm going to get to the bottom of all the sexual shenanigans in this house.

(**CASEY** *has now pushed* **COTT** *off R. and turns back towards* **FRED** *and* **GLADYS**.)

FRED. I think we should talk about the chamber dear. Don't you think so Mrs. Adams?

CASEY. I suppose we could.

GLADYS. Now Mrs. Adams, please sit down. (**FRED** *sits on the couch L. side,* **GLADYS** *R. side, as* **CASEY** *sits in the chair.*) So, let's begin right at the beginning. What do you think it was that got everything started?

CASEY. I suppose it's a build up of pressure.

GLADYS. What?

CASEY. It seems if you haven't used it for a while, the pressure builds up.

GLADYS. What? Fred, what does that mean?

FRED. Well dear –

GLADYS. Don't answer that, I don't think I want to know.

FRED. I think Mrs. Adams is talking about –

GLADYS. I know what Mrs. Adams is talking about. It's (*She turns L. to* **FRED**, *away from* **CASEY** *and whispers.*) carnal desires.

FRED. But dear –

GLADYS. Now Mrs. Adams, we really do need to have a sensible adult conversation.

CASEY. O.K.

GLADYS. Now, how do you think we can get it stopped?

CASEY. Stopped?

GLADYS. Yes, we can't allow it to go on you know.

CASEY. Why not? It's really quite beneficial. I mean afterwards, you feel real happy and relaxed.

GLADYS. Oh – Oh – Oh! Fred!

CASEY. Yes, now that everything seems to be functioning naturally and normally, I might try it myself later.

GLADYS. Oh – Oh – Oh!!

FRED. Gladys dear, I think what Mrs. Adams is talking about is –

GLADYS. I know what she's talking about. I can hear her. Mrs. Adams, let me try again. Do I take it that you approve of this?

CASEY. Well, I didn't at first, but I believe I do now. I mean, the first time I tried it my skirt flew over my head, and I didn't like it very much, but now that the pressure has been relieved, everybody seems to be enjoying it.

GLADYS. Well, I most certainly don't want to enjoy it, and I won't have Fred enjoying it either.

CASEY. Perhaps you'd like it better if you did it together.

GLADYS. I can assure you I most certainly do not intend to do it at all, if I can help it.

CASEY. Oh well, I suppose I could do it with Mr. McNicoll, if you like.

GLADYS. I have never heard of anything so outrageous in my life.

CASEY. Really? I'm sorry you feel that way. It's not really any big deal either way.

GLADYS. It's time like this, I feel I skipped an entire generation. There will be no more talk of you and Fred doing it together.

CASEY. O.K.

GLADYS. Now, it's about Nanny.

CASEY. What about her?

GLADYS. Well, Mr. Brooks seems very eager, but it is clear that Nanny is unwilling.

CASEY. That's right. You see Nanny has all these physical problems, and she absolutely refuses to have anything to do with it.

GLADYS. Well, good for Nanny. I agree with her completely. I only wish I could refuse to have anything to do with it.

CASEY. But she did say it might be good for her rheumatism if she could do it lying down, but standing up was out of the question.

GLADYS. Standing up? Oh – Oh – Oh –

(*She staggers to her feet, and pretends to faint, as* **FRED** *stands and catches her.*)

(*Enter* **BEN** *from the kitchen, now wearing the large apron.*)

CASEY. Excuse me. (*She stands and meets* **BEN** *by the counter.*) Ben, I've had it. You talk to Mrs. McNicoll for a bit.

BEN. What about?

CASEY. I don't know, anything. Tell her about your cooking lessons. (*Exit to the kitchen.*)

GLADYS. (*Sees* **BEN** *and quickly recovers.*) Young man, come and sit down.

(**BEN** *sits in the chair, and* **GLADYS** *resumes her seat on the couch R. side, as* **FRED** *sits on the couch L. side.*)

I want to talk to you about your relationship with Sue the chef. You can't fool me you know. Now, what is going on?

BEN. Well, actually, most of it is happening in the kitchen.

GLADYS. What?

BEN. Yes. That's where we're doing it.

GLADYS. In the kitchen?

BEN. Yes. I'm learning a lot. You see, she's been specially trained, and I've discovered I'm not really very good at it.

GLADYS. Specially trained?

BEN. Yes, they lay great emphasis on the basics. For example, preparation is the key to everything.

GLADYS. Preparation? Oh – Oh – Oh, I think I'm going to faint again. Stand by Fred.

BEN. It's very important to start to do several things at the same time so that everything finishes at the same time.

GLADYS. Oh – Oh – Oh! Fred, are you standing by?

FRED. (*Stands.*) Standing by.

GLADYS. I'm not sure we should be having this conversation.

BEN. But you said you wanted to talk about it.

GLADYS. Well I did, but this is very inappropriate.

BEN. I don't think so. I'm getting some real hands on experience. (*Gladys reacts.*) I mean I've never met anyone willing to give me lessons before.

GLADYS. Oh – Oh – Oh!

BEN. She actually allows me to handle some things on my own. I find that very exciting.

GLADYS. Well stop! We don't want anyone getting excited. Do we Fred.

FRED. No dear, shall I sit down now?

(**GLADYS** *nods, and he sits.*)

BEN. Well, perhaps excited was a slight exaggeration, but I have to tell you, I am really enjoying the experience.

FRED. I can almost remember when I used to enjoy the experience too.

GLADYS. Fred!

FRED. Sorry dear.

(*Enter* **BROOKS** *from U.L. He peers cautiously into the room, sees Nanny is not there, and enters.*)

BEN. (*Seizes the opportunity to escape.*) Excuse me. (*Exits to the kitchen.*)

GLADYS. Ah, there you are Mr. Brooks. Please sit down. Fred and I would like to talk to you.

FRED. We would?

GLADYS. Yes, we would.

BROOKS. (*Sits on the chair*) What would you like to talk about?

GLADYS. We'd like to talk to you about Nanny.

BROOKS. What about Nanny?

GLADYS. Well, don't you think you're a bit old for that sort of thing?

BROOKS. Oh come now, Mrs. McNicoll, we're never too old for that.

GLADYS. Oh – oh – I think I'm going to faint. Fred, I think you should end this conversation.

FRED. Me? I haven't ever been in this conversation.

GLADYS. Are you arguing Fred?

FRED. No dear, I was thinking about... (*He gazes into space*)

GLADYS. Are you going to tell us?

FRED. Oh yes. (*There is a long pause while* **FRED** *continues to gaze wistfully into space.*)

GLADYS. Will it be today? Oh! Oh! I do believe the chamber set you off.

(*Enter* **SUE** *from the kitchen. She is wearing the short apron and shuffles a little to keep facing D.S.*)

SUE. We've got your clothes dried Mr. McNicoll. They're all ready in the laundry room. Perhaps you'd like to change.

FRED. (*Gets up*) Thank you I would.

GLADYS. Are you sure they're properly dried?

SUE. I think so. Would you like to check them?

GLADYS. (*Gets up and moves R.*) Yes, I would. Come on Fred. (*They exit R. to the kitchen*)

SUE. (*Crosses L. behind the chair to above the couch*) You know Mr. Brooks, you've really surprised everyone this evening.

BROOKS. What do you mean?

SUE. You know what I mean – Nanny!

BROOKS. Oh, Nanny. Well, you know, perhaps I got a little carried away.

SUE. I got carried away once.

BROOKS. You did?

SUE. Yes. I was on the wrong bus and ended up in Milwaukee.

BROOKS. I see. Talking of Nanny. Do you know where she is? (*He gets up and looks around*)

SUE. Last time I saw her she was in the control room.

BROOKS. Right I'll just see if she needs any help. (*Runs off R. into the kitchen.*)

SUE. That's probably not a very sensible thing to – (*But* **BROOKS** *has gone.*)

(**GLADYS** *and* **FRED** *enter from the kitchen.* **FRED** *is carrying his clothes over his arm. Once again Gladys's mouth is in constant motion.*)

GLADYS. And next time do be more careful about going in that bathroom.

FRED. But I –

GLADYS. I don't want to hear any more. You really have been in a very truculent mood this evening. Just because I gave you the power over the remote system doesn't mean – (*They exit to bedroom 2 and close the door*)

(*There's a yell from* **COTT** *off R. followed by a dull thud, followed by a long agonized groan from* **BROOKS**. **COTT** *enters from the kitchen with a large wooden meat-tenderizing mallet in his hand. He comes L. towards* **SUE**.)

COTT. I'm going to kill him.

SUE. (*Laughs*) I can't say I blame you.

COTT. You know he could grope for America. He doesn't let up, and what the heck is it about my feet? (*He slumps down on the couch R. side*) I mean look at them.

SUE. They're just irresistible.

COTT. Yeah! Yeah! Yeah!

BROOKS. (*Off*) Nanny, where are you?

COTT. Oh Lord, I can't face him again. Give me a hand will you.

(**COTT** *takes the afghan from the back of the couch and motions to* **SUE** *to crouch down behind the couch. He slumps down and* **SUE** *pulls the afghan over his head. We now see Sue's head and Cott's feet looking like one* *body. Sue's arms are exposed holding the afghan up to her chin.* COTT *still has the mallet in his hand under the afghan. Enter* BROOKS *from R. in the kitchen.)*

BROOKS. Ah, Mrs. Adams.

(SUE *looks around, then realizes he means her*)

Have you seen Nanny?

SUE. Well – er – not recently.

BROOKS. That's strange, I thought I saw her come in here.

SUE. You know, I really don't think that Nanny appreciates your advances.

BROOKS. I suppose you're right, it's just that I find her so very attractive, especially her feet.

(*Cott's boots tap the floor as* BROOKS *comes D.R. and now sees "Sue's" feet*)

and talking of feet, has anyone ever told you what beautiful feet you have.

SUE. Mr. Brooks! Cut it out. You're old enough to be my father.

BROOKS. (*Staring at the feet as* COTT *crosses and uncrosses his legs in a very "unladylike" manner with the knees well apart*) I know. I'm sorry, but your feet remind me of Nanny. (*He sits on the couch R. side*)

(*Enter* BEN *from the kitchen now wearing the long apron.*)

BEN. Hi Sue, have you seen –

(BROOKS *has placed his hand on "Sue's" right knee, but turns to look at* BEN, *as* COTT, *with the mallet in his left hand reaches out from under the afghan and hits the back of Brook's hand, then returns the mallet under the afghan.*)

BROOKS. Oh – oh – oh!

SUE. Is something wrong?

BROOKS. My hand! My hand!

SUE. Oh my! Did we by any chance put it somewhere it wasn't supposed to be?

BEN. (*Now seeing the feet for the first time*) What's going on?

BROOKS. Your wife hit my hand.

BEN. My wife? Oh yes, that's right, my wife. Why would she hit your hand?

SUE. That's a very good question darling. Why don't you answer it Mr. Brooks?

BROOKS. Well – er – well – er – I think I'll go and lie down for a bit. (*Exit to bedroom 1.*)

(**SUE** *lowers the afghan and she and* **COTT** *stand up*)

SUE. You really whacked him this time.

COTT. I don't care. He deserves it.

(*Enter* **CASEY** *from the kitchen.*)

CASEY. What are you guys all doing standing around out here? Where are Godzilla and Pussy Cat?

SUE. They're in their room, changing.

CASEY. O.K. Listen up everyone. I think it's going quite well. As far as I can see, Mr. and Mrs. McNicoll seem to quite like this house, so, we need Nanny and Chef to disappear for awhile so Ben can get to work on his sales pitch. Right Ben?

BEN. I'm supposed to sell this house looking like this? (*He turns to face U.S. and we see his boxers again*)

CASEY. We've got Mr. McNicoll's clothes dried, he's changing right now. You can wear the jeans again.

SUE. But what about me? I can't spend the whole evening like this. (*She turns away so* **CASEY** *and the audience sees her undies*)

CASEY. (*Laughs*) Oh, I don't know, maybe you should dress like that all the time. It would drive your boyfriend crazy.

SUE. I haven't got a boyfriend.

CASEY. You soon would have, if you dressed like that. O.K. you guys, let's get you out of here. Wait in the master bedroom. As soon as I get them, I'll bring the jeans for you Ben.

(**SUE** *and* **BEN** *exit to the master bedroom as* **CASEY** *re-arranges the afghan on the back of the couch.*)

O.K., now is everything working as it should?

COTT. You've got to be kidding! I've got this enlarged prostate which makes going to the bathroom a very painful experience, and my digestive tract keeps having these seizures –

CASEY. I meant is everything working in the house.

COTT. Oh, you've still got to be kidding.

CASEY. Let me rephrase that. Is everything working as well as you can get it working?

COTT Well, the air pressure seems about right, if that's what you mean?

CASEY. O.K. that's good. Where's Brooks and what's happening with him?

COTT. He's gone to lie down, and I think perhaps he might just keep his hands to himself from now on.

(*Enter* **FRED** *from bedroom 2, now wearing his original suit, and carrying the blue jeans, a brochure and a remote.*)

FRED. Oh hi Mrs. Adams, hi Nanny.

CASEY. Is everything alright?

FRED. Just fine, thanks. I brought you the jeans back. (*Hands them to* **CASEY**.)

CASEY. Thank you. (*She turns to* **COTT**) Nanny, don't you have things to do?

COTT. No.

CASEY. (*Glares at him*) Nanny!

COTT. Oh, yes, right. I've got things to do. (*Whispers to* **CASEY**) What have I got to do?

CASEY. Why don't you take Mr. Adams the blue jeans? (*She hands them to him*)

COTT. Right. (*He exits L. to the master bedroom*)

CASEY. You really seem to be enjoying the remote systems.

FRED. I am actually. I've figured out that sometimes when you press a combination of different numbers, things kind of speed up.

CASEY. Really. I didn't know that.

FRED. Yeah. Watch the closet. Ready?

CASEY. O.K.

(**FRED** *clicks the remote and the closet does its thing, in and out at breakneck speed*)

FRED. What do you think of that?

CASEY. It's O.K. I suppose, but why would you want it to go that fast?

FRED. Oh, I don't know. It might be useful sometime.

CASEY. Well, if you'll excuse me, I really do have things to do in the kitchen.

(**FRED** *is left alone on stage reading his brochure and clicking his remote. He talks to himself*)

FRED. Now, let me see if I lower it about two feet. (*He measures with his hands and presses buttons on the remote*) That should be about right.

(*He turns around the room clicking. The fridge door opens and closes. The fireplace does it bang routine. We hear the noise of the trash system. He approaches it cautiously, takes a handkerchief out of his pocket and dangles it over the receptacle. It is snatched out of his hand and disappears. He clicks and the noise stops*)

BEN. (*Enters from U.L. now wearing the jeans.*) Hi Mr. McNicoll, how's it going? How do you feel about the house?

FRED. Well, it takes a little getting used to, but as long as my wife stays determined to make me work everything, I'm beginning to really like it.

BEN. Excellent! You know for all the features it has, it really is priced to sell.

FRED. I know that, you don't have to sell me on the house. I really like it. I'd just like a little more time to play around with the remote system if you don't mind.

BEN. Not at all, please, take all the time you want

FRED. Thank you.

COTT. (*Enters from U.L. and looks nervously around.*) Has anybody seen Brooks?

FRED. Not for a little while, so my guess would be he's in his room.

COTT. Thank heaven for that.

FRED. He really seems to have found a special place in his heart for you Nanny.

COTT. Yes, and I've got a special place in my heart for him. It's somewhere between an I.R.S. auditor and hemorrhoids.

BEN. Mr. McNicoll was just telling me how he is enjoying all the remote systems in the house.

COTT. Good. Mr. McNicoll, may I ask you something?

FRED. Of course Nanny.

COTT. Well, you've met Mr. Brooks, now I ask you, what is the problem with my feet?

(*They all look at the his feet.*)

FRED. Perhaps if you wore different shoes?

COTT. I can't wear any other shoes. You see, I've got carbuncles, the size of grapes, on every toe but one, and that one has a genetic ulcerated corn, the size of an egg, which I inherited from my parents.

FRED. (*Laughing.*) Maybe Mr. Brooks would be discouraged if you showed him your bare feet?

COTT. Show Brooks my bare feet? You've got to be kidding.

FRED. (*Laughing.*) I guess you're right, that might drive him crazy. Let's face it Nanny, some of us have it, and some of us don't. You must feel so selfish, having so much of it.

COTT. I don't want any of it.

BEN. Nanny, why don't you go back to our room, and keep Sue—I mean my wife—I mean the chef company. Mr.

McNicoll wants to experiment with some of the remote numbers.

COTT. I think I will. These shooting pains in my legs are really giving me fits. (*He wanders off L.*) I wonder if you can get shin splints in your thighs? I bet that's it. I'm the first person in the world with thigh splints. (*Exits U.L.*)

FRED. (*Laughs.*) She really is quite a character isn't she? Certainly not what you would call a typical American.

BEN. Oh, she's not American, she's from Wisconsin.

FRED. Very funny!

BROOKS. (*Enters from bedroom 1.*) Oh, hello. Has anyone seen Nanny?

BEN. Really Mr. Brooks, if you are a reasonable human being, and I use that term loosely, don't you think you should leave Nanny alone.

BROOKS. Maybe a more subtle approach might be better.

BEN. So far you've been about as subtle as a loaded colt 45.

BROOKS. I'll bet I know exactly where she is. (*He runs off U.L.*) Oh Nannykins, I'm coming—

BEN AND FRED. (*Counting together*) One – two – three.

(*There is a yell from* COTT, *followed by a dull thud, followed by an agonizing groan from* BROOKS. COTT *enters jauntily from U.L., the meat tenderizer mallet in his hand, and a big silly grin on his face. He crosses R. and exits to the kitchen. He is followed by* SUE, *who hurries after him.*)

SUE. I don't think you should have done that Nanny. (*Exit R. to the kitchen*)

BROOKS. (*Now appears in the archway. U.L. He is leaning on the wall, bent over double and his hands on his crotch.*) OOOW – OOOW.

FRED. It looks like he's been hit right in the gentlemen's department.

BEN. Again!

BROOKS. I think I'll go back and lie down. (*He staggers off U.L.*)

GLADYS. (*Appears in the doorway of bedroom 2.*) Fred. Where are you? Ah, there you are, what have you been up to? You there young man, I want to talk to you.

BEN. Me?

GLADYS. Yes, of course you. Do you see any other young men? Fred, I'll be right out, have your brochure handy, and the remote ready. (*She turns back into bedroom 2, leaving the door open.*)

FRED. Would you mind leaving my wife and I alone for a few minutes please?

BEN. You want to be alone with her? I'm sorry, that wasn't called for.

FRED. That's all right, I'm kind of used to it. She wasn't always like this you know.

BEN. No?

FRED. She once was Miss Congeniality at the Cheese Castle pageant.

BEN. Really? Well, I hope you don't mind if I don't bow down and curtsey before the Dairy Queen of Wisconsin.

FRED. That's O.K. Just give us a few minutes.

BEN. My pleasure. (*Exit R. to the kitchen.*)

GLADYS. (*Enters from bedroom 2. Her mouth in constant motion.*) Where's that Adams fellow? I told him I wanted to talk to him. Why isn't he here?

    (**FRED** *opens his mouth to say something, but never gets a word out.*)

    And another thing, why is he always hanging around that chef person? I'm beginning to think there is some hanky panky going on here, (*She has come D.R. towards the closet and points to it*) and all these gadgets, do we really need them?

FRED. Well dear –

GLADYS. I mean they're all well and good, but they don't look very nice. I mean would some of our antiques fit in with all this modern stuff? What about my antique teapot? You remember my mother's teapot, don't you Fred?

FRED. You mean the one that originally belonged to a civil war general, was stolen by a carpet-bagger, lost for two generations, then found by your great uncle's mistress, who bequeathed it to your grandmother?

GLADYS. No, not that one. You know, I'm just not sure about the ion chamber, does it really work? Look at it. It looks like we're storing grain in the living room. Why couldn't they have made it square like everything else in the world?

FRED. Well dear, it's probably because of the air system.

GLADYS. Nonsense, and don't interrupt me, you know I don't like that.

(*Fred sighs and rolls his eyes heavenward. At this point* **GLADYS** *is standing away from the R. wall level with the closet door facing L.* **FRED** *grins to the audience and unseen by* **GLADYS** *clicks his remote. The arm comes out, but it is now only about two feet off the ground. There is a coat draped over the rail. The finger hits* **GLADYS** *in the derriere and she falls slightly backwards.*)

Oh – oh – oh (*She is now firmly impaled on the finger*)

FRED. Is something wrong dear?

GLADYS. Oh – oh – get me off this thing.

FRED. (*Pretending to click the remote, but clearly not doing so*) It seems to have gone wrong dear.

GLADYS. Oh – oh – oh (*Trying to get up*)

(*Enter* **SUE** *from the kitchen, now wearing the long apron.*)

SUE. What's wrong, I heard this noise. (*Sees* **GLADYS**) Oh goodness, let me help.

(**SUE** *comes D.R. to help* **GLADYS**, *but falls over the arm. As she falls nearly on top of* **GLADYS**, *she grabs the coat. It gets pulled over Gladys's head. They both become hopelessly entangled in the coat.*)

GLADYS. Oh – oh – Fred, do something, oh – oh get this thing off me. Oh – oh – Fred, what are you doing? Where are you? Oh – oh – oh –

(*They both eventually end up on the floor, but* **GLADYS** *is now free of the arm*)

Fred, did you do that? Get rid of that thing.

(**FRED** *now clicks the remote and the arm withdraws and the closet door closes*)

Oh – it grabbed me by the buttocks!

FRED. Are you alright dear?

GLADYS. Do I look alright? What sort of question is that? Here, help me sit down. (*She goes to sit on the trash disposal unit.*)

SUE. I don't think you should sit there.

GLADYS. Don't tell me where to sit. I'll sit wherever I please, won't I Fred?

FRED. I think what she meant was –

GLADYS. I know what she meant. I don't need you to tell me, just let me catch my breath for a minute. (*Sits on the disposal unit*)

SUE. It might help if you quit talking.

GLADYS. What was that?

SUE. I said, I got to do a bit of walking! To the kitchen that is.

(**SUE** *gives* **FRED** *a friendly smile and exits R. to the kitchen.* **FRED** *watches her go, grins and unseen by* **GLADYS** *clicks his remote. The whirring noise of the trash disposal starts up.* **GLADYS** *shifts her position a little, but is unable to move. She twists and turns, but she is firmly stuck on the contraption.*)

GLADYS. Oh dear. I seem to be stuck. Oh my goodness. I feel quite peculiar. Oh – oh – oh. (*This last series of "ohs" gives the impression she might even be enjoying the experience*)

FRED. Is something wrong dear?

GLADYS. Something is definitely wrong. I don't seem to be able to move. Fred, are you responsible for this?

FRED. (*Clearly enjoying himself.*) Me dear?

GLADYS. What is that noise? Take that big stupid grin off your face and help me get up.

(**FRED** *puts the remote down on the counter and pretends to help her*)

This is most distressing, what is wrong with this stool?

FRED. You don't seem to be coming free dear.

GLADYS. I don't understand what's happening, my dress seems to be caught in something. (*They continue to struggle*) Fred, I know this is your fault.

FRED. Why would it be my fault?

GLADYS. I can tell by that look on your face. Oh for heaven's sake, go and get some help.

FRED. Very well dear, just stay there while I find someone.

GLADYS. Do I look as though I'm going anywhere?

(*As* **FRED** *exits R. to the kitchen, he slides the remote R. on the counter so as to be sure* **GLADYS** *can't reach it.* **GLADYS** *continues to struggle*)

Oh – oh – oh! (*Left alone on stage, Gladys continues her gyrations, this time, clearly enjoying the experience*). Oh my goodness!

(**FRED** *returns immediately with* **SUE** *from the kitchen, picks up the remote and puts it in his pocket.*)

FRED. Perhaps between us we can get her off. (*They try to lift* **GLADYS**, *but to no avail*)

SUE. It's no good. I think you're going to have to take your dress off.

GLADYS. I shall do no such thing.

SUE. You know I once got stuck in a seat like that.

FRED. Really? How?

SUE. Well, I was on this bus going to visit my sister in Green Bay, and someone had spilled crazy glue on the seat, and I couldn't move.

FRED. Good heavens! What happened?

SUE. I ripped my dress trying to get free, and never did get to my sister's.

FRED. Why not?

SUE. Turns out I was on the wrong bus and ended up in Milwaukee.

GLADYS. If I may interrupt this little tête-à-tête, I would like to remind you that I am in a very uncomfortable and compromising position. My posterior seems to be slowly sinking into the depths of an abyss the likes of which only the most perverted of souls would ever want to know, and you stand there talking about bus service in Milwaukee. Fred, I've told you before, there is nothing even slightly humorous in this situation, so get that big, silly smile off your face!

FRED. Well dear, you heard the lady, you're going to have to take your dress off.

GLADYS. Very well. Fred, go in the kitchen, I don't want you seeing me in my unmentionables, it might set you off again. (**SUE** *raises her eyebrows to the heavens*)

FRED. Very well dear. (*He exits to the kitchen taking his remote with him.*)

(**SUE** *and* **GLADYS** *start to get Gladys' dress off. They get it partially off, but* **SUE** *has one of her arms in one of the sleeves. They twist and turn, but become hopelessly tangled. Eventually they stop struggling.*)

SUE. Help, someone, anyone, Help! (**CASEY** *and* **COTT** *enter from the kitchen*) Could you give us a hand please, we seem to be stuck. (**CASEY** *goes to help but nothing much happens*)

CASEY. Nanny, give us a hand please.

COTT. I would, but you see I have this phlebitis in my lower legs, and if I exert myself I'm liable to have blood clots moving all over, and I could be gone, just like that.

CASEY. How in heavens name did you manage this?

GLADYS. It's not me, it's her. She's a living, walking, breathing disaster area.

CASEY. I know. I think the vibration from all those bus rides must have loosened her brain.

SUE. (*Looking rather hurt*) I was only trying to help.

CASEY. I know, it's just that every time you try to help, (**SUE** *looks like she's about to cry*) never mind, I'm sure you're doing your best.

GLADYS. Excuse me, but if you two are finished with your mutual admiration society, I'd like some help – today!

COTT. Wait a minute. Who's got a remote?

GLADYS. Fred has one.

CASEY. O.K. let me find him. Nanny, there's a robe in the master bedroom, would you get it for Mrs. McNicoll please.

(**CASEY** *exits R. to the kitchen.* **COTT** *exits U.L. Immediately there is a repeat of the sequence as before. A yell from* **COTT**, *a dull thud and an agonized groan from* **BROOKS**, *who now appears in the U.L. archway holding his crotch. He staggers R. gives* **GLADYS** *and* **SUE** *a little finger wave as he passes them and exits to the kitchen.* **COTT** *enters carrying a robe as* **CASEY** *and* **FRED** *return from the kitchen.*)

CASEY. Can you switch this thing off ?

FRED. I suppose so.

(*He clicks the remote and* **GLADYS** *and* **SUE** *fall off the disposal unit. They pick themselves up. Gladys' dress is now around her ankles. She is wearing the most unglamorous underwear imaginable, enormous bloomers, which reach from her waist to well below her knees, and a large corset. She steps out of her dress.* **CASEY** *takes the robe from* **COTT** *and hands it to* **GLADYS**, *who puts it on.* **CASEY** *and* **COTT** *exit to the kitchen.*)

GLADYS. I have never been so humiliated in all my life. Fred, why didn't you switch that thing off earlier?

FRED. Well dear, I wasn't sure –

GLADYS. You're supposed to be sure. I'm not at all certain you're to be trusted with that thing.

(*Enter* **BEN** *from the kitchen. He sees* **GLADYS** *and starts "twitching."*)

GLADYS. Ah, there you are young man. I wanted to talk to you. Where did you get to?

BEN. (*Grins at* **FRED.**) I – er – I had to go and get some of my twitching medication.

GLADYS. Well, don't disappear again. I need to get properly dressed, and then young man, we are going to have a discussion about what is going on in this house. (*She looks at her dress on the floor.*)

(**FRED** *"gets the message" and picks it up. They exit to bedroom 2, leaving the door open.*)

(**SUE** *and* **BEN** *move D. R. below the counter.*)

SUE. Oh dear, that doesn't sound very positive.

BEN. Oh, I don't know. I have a feeling that maybe Fred has things under control.

SUE. Fred?

BEN. Yes. I get the distinct impression that he's not quite as docile as he appears to be.

SUE. You mean there's a chance they might buy the house? (*Flings her arms around him and kisses him on the lips*) Oh that's wonderful, that would pay off most of my student loans.

(*They embrace again, as* **GLADYS** *peeks out of the door of bedroom 2 and sees them.*)

(**GLADYS** *ducks back into bedroom 2, as* **COTT** *enters from the kitchen. He is carrying a length of coiled rope with a loop at one end, and a set of jumper cables.* **BEN** *and* **SUE** *hold their embrace and watch as* **COTT** *removes the light bulb from the light fixture on the wall above the fireplace and plugs one end of the jumper cables into the socket. Then with the rope behind his back he sits at the L. end of the couch and positions his feet in a pathetic attempt at a sexy pose.*)

COTT. Oh Mr. Broosky – Wooksy, your little naughty Nanny is waiting for you. Where are you Brooksy-Wooksy?

(**BROOKS** *enters from the kitchen, sees* **COTT** *and advances lustfully, his arms outstretched in front of him. He comes D.L. and makes a move to grab Cott's "balloons." Quick as a flash* **COTT** *gets the loop of the rope over Brooks's hands, tightens the noose, pushes him down on the couch and hog-ties his legs. He then takes the jumper cables, holds one clamp in each hand and raises them in the air. He is just about to apply them to Brooks's crotch, when* **GLADYS** *appears from bedroom 2, still wearing the robe, followed by* **FRED**.)

BROOKS. AIEOUGGGH!

GLADYS. Nanny! What do you think you're doing? I'm shocked.

COTT. Not nearly as much as he's going to be.

GLADYS. Stop that immediately.

COTT. Not on your life.

BROOKS. AEIOUGGGH! Help!

(*Enter* **CASEY** *on the dead run from the kitchen.*)

CASEY. Stop! (*She rushes over to restrain* **COTT** *and manages to get the jumper cables away from him.*) What's going on here?

BEN. Excuse us.

(**BEN** *and* **SUE** *shuffle off to the kitchen, as* **FRED** *sits on the L. stool.*)

GLADYS. I'll tell you what's going on here. I just saw Mr. Adams here, (*She moves R. to the edge of the counter.*) kissing the chef. What do you think of that? Just as soon as I get dressed, I'll be right out. There's definitely something weird happening here and I intend to find out what it is.

(**FRED** *has followed* **GLADYS** *R. and quietly opens the door of the ion chamber. He pretends to bump into* **GLADYS** *and she falls into the chamber as* **FRED** *clicks his remote and the door closes.*)

CASEY. (*Looking curiously at* **FRED**.) Nanny, why don't you leave us alone?

(**COTT** *obviously thinking about the jumper cables again, opens his mouth to protest.*)

NANNY!

(**COTT** *shrugs and exits to the kitchen.*)

(**CASEY** *starts to untie* **BROOKS**. **FRED** *clicks his remote and the ion chamber door opens.* **GLADYS** *has obviously never stopped talking.*)

GLADYS. I do believe there are lascivious undertakings happening right under our very noses, and let me assure everyone that I – (**FRED** *clicks and the door closes*)

(**CASEY** *has now freed* **BROOKS** *who gets up.*)

BROOKS. Thank you. Which way did Nanny go?

CASEY. I don't believe it. Don't you ever give up?

BROOKS. (*Ignores her and moves off R.*) I know you're in there Nanny, this is Brooksy-Wooksy. I'm coming. (*Exit R. into the kitchen*)

CASEY Aren't you going to let her out?

FRED. Probably not. Let's see if she's stopped talking. (*He clicks and the door opens*)

GLADYS. – – – and I'm going to make it my personal business to find out just what lewd affairs are taking place, and what's more – –

(**FRED** *clicks and the door closes.*)

FRED. Let's give her another minute, maybe she'll wind down a little.

CASEY. You can't just leave her in there.

FRED. (*Smiling*) Why not?

CASEY. Well, because – (*She pauses*) Oooh! You're really enjoying this aren't you?

FRED. I love it!

(*There is a repeat of the off stage* **COTT** *and* **BROOKS** *rountine. A yell from* **COTT**, *a dull thud, followed by the groan from* **BROOKS**. **CASEY** *who is still L. by the couch and* **FRED**, *sitting at the counter, watch as* **BROOKS**

backs L. out of the kitchen. He is bent over and hold-
ing his crotch. He is followed by **COTT** *brandishing an*
enormous pair of log tongs. **BROOKS** *backs away D.R.*
towards the front door.)

BROOKS. Help, can anybody help, look at her, she's mad,
she really means it.

CASEY. Mr. McNicoll can you do something?

FRED. Sure.

(**FRED** *clicks the remote and the closet door opens. The*
arm appears at the three foot level and impales **BROOKS**
from the rear. **FRED** *clicks again and* **BROOKS,** *yelling*
all the time, is dragged off into the closet and the door
closes.)

COTT. Darn it. I nearly had him

CASEY. (*To Fred*) Thank you.

FRED. You're welcome.

(*He clicks and the ion chamber door opens.* **GLADYS**
doesn't let up for a second)

GLADYS. (*Steps out*) – – and what's more, if I didn't have
to use the bathroom immediately, I would definitely
be getting to the bottom of all this So don't anybody
think they're off the hook. Fred, you wait out here for
a minute. I'll be right back. (*Exit to bathroom closing the*
door)

(**FRED** *strolls nonchalantly up to the door, leans on the*
wall, grins to everyone and very deliberately pushes the
self-cleaning button. The red light starts flashing.)

(**BEN,** *now wearing the jeans, and* **SUE** *enter from the*
kitchen.)

BEN. What in heavens name was all that noise?

CASEY. Mr. Brooks decided to hang it all up.

SUE. Why are we cleaning the bathroom again?

FRED. Mrs. McNicoll, is making a clean break.

BEN. I have absolutely no idea what is going on.

CASEY. Perhaps Mr. McNicoll, would care to explain,

FRED. There's really very little to explain. I know you must all be wondering about Mrs. McNicoll, and how she seems to treat people badly. I know she gets carried away a bit sometimes, but, she really doesn't mean anyone any harm, in fact, inside, she's really a very kind and generous person. The bottom line I suppose, is that I doubt if she will ever be willing to learn how to operate the house of the future. Which leaves me in a kind of nice place. (*He holds up the remote and grins.*)

(*The red light stops flashing, the buzzer sounds and, the bathroom door opens and* **GLADYS** *staggers out. She is soaking wet from head to foot.*)

GLADYS. Fred –

FRED. I'd like you to be quiet Gladys.

(**GLADYS** *opens her mouth to say something, but* **FRED** *silences her, by raising his finger and giving her an icy stare.*)

You've said quite enough for one day. By the way you guys, congratulations, we will be buying this house.

(**GLADYS** *opens her mouth to say something*)

Won't we Gladys?

GLADYS. (*Looks at him for a second*) Yes dear.

(**SUE** *and* **BEN** *embrace and kiss each other.* **COTT** *and* **CASEY** *"high five" and:*)

CURTAIN

AUTHOR'S NOTES ON THE TECHNICAL ASPECTS OF "THE HOUSE OF THE FUTURE" No mechanical or electronic devices are needed. All the " gadgets" are carefully designed to be operated manually by off-stage crew members.

1. THE CLOSET simply needs a rail (or perhaps two at different levels) which are pushed out on stage by a hidden crew member and withdrawn the same way.

2. THE TRASH DISPOSAL should have a top with a grating, which will enable Ben and Gladys to sit on it without falling in, and a hole in the center large enough to "swallow" Ben's pants and the broken dishes. This is achieved by a crew member sitting behind the counter with one arm reaching into the disposal unit, which can be constructed as part of the counter or an attachment to it, like this

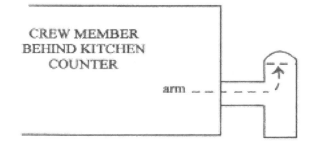

3. THE FRIDGE DOOR would need a simple rod, attached to the bottom of it, which enables a crew member to open and close it from behind.

4. THE ION CHAMBER can be tubular or square. Tubular would look more authentic, but if this construction proves difficult, it could be rectangular with a simple sliding door. If rectangular, then Gladys's lines about it looking like a grain storage unit would be deleted.

An off-stage crew could work the door, giving the impression of an automatic door operated by the remotes. If this is too difficult, the script is carefully written to enable cast members to open and close the door manually.

No technical director should be apprehensive about any of the innovations of "the house of the future." The plot, in any event, is all about these gadgets going wrong. So, if something did go wrong, it would almost certainly add to the humor.

Page 24. SUE's hair "standing straight up in the air" is, of course, a wig, which she discards in the second or two she collapses behind the kitchen counter.

Page 34. CASEY will also need a similar wig.

Page 45, 55. If the relative sizes of the actors playing the roles of COTT, BEN, and FRED are such that they really couldn't all wear Cott's jeans, the author does not recommend "cheating" on the sizes, but sees humor in that situation.

FURNITURE AND PROPERTY LIST

ON STAGE
Sofa with 2 cushions and an afghan.
Low back chair.
Coffee table.
Wall mounted lamp.
2 bar stools.
Kitchen counter. On it: a peppermill.
Kitchen cabinets. In them: Wine glasses. Water glasses.
Fridge. In it: Water pitcher. Wine bottle.
Trash disposal attached to the kitchen counter.
Fire place with mantel. On it: A vase.
"Happy birthday" sign.
Decorative balloons.

ACT 1. OFFSTAGE
Cardboard box. In it: Brochures and 4 remotes. (BROADBENT)
Overnight case. (CASEY)
"Closet of the future" arm, with coathangers.
Cardboard box. In it: Wrapped food & groceries. (SUE)
Cardboard box. (COTT)
Compressed air cylinder. (COTT)
2 broken plates. (SUE)
Tool belt with screwdriver. (COTT)
Spiked up wig. (SUE)
Spiked up wig. (CASEY)
Umbrella. (GLADYS)
2 large suitcases. (FRED)
Plastic bag. (CASEY)
Meat tenderizing mallet. (COTT)
Coat in the "closet of the future."

ACT 11. OFFSTAGE
Tray with cups, saucers, coffee pot. (CASEY)
Tray with cake, cake knife, desert forks, plates. (BEN)
Bolt cutters. (COTT)
Rope. (COTT)
Jumper cables. (COTT)
Log tongs. (COTT)
Robe. (COTT *for* GLADYS)

PERSONAL
GLADYS. Black soot make-up.
FRED. Handkerchief.

COSTUMES

BEN	Sport jacket	**GLADYS**	Winter coat
	Dress pants		Gloves
	Shirt with short sleeves		Scarf
	Shoes & socks		Boots
	Boxer shorts		Dress
			Bloomers & top
BROADBENT	Business suit		Corset
	Shirt & tie		2 robes, one wet, one dry
	Shoes & socks		
	Overcoat		
	Scarf	**FRED**	Overcoat
	Hat		Hat
			Gloves
CASEY	Winter coat		2 business suits, one wet, one dry
	Skirt		Shirt
	Sweater		Tie
	Boots		Dress shoes
	Ski hat		
	Lacy underwear		
SUE	Winter coat	**BROOKS**	Overcoat
	Boots		Hat
	Ski hat		Scarf
	Sweater		Business suit
	Blouse with short sleeves		Shirt
	Scarf		Tie
	Wrap around skirt		Dress shoes
	Lacy underwear		
	Large apron		
	Small apron		
MR COTT	Overcoat		
	Blue jeans		
	Work shirt }*Same*		
	Woman's blouse }*material*		
	Boots		
	Red socks		
	Baseball cap		
	Skirt		
	Wig with hair rollers		
	"Bosoms"		

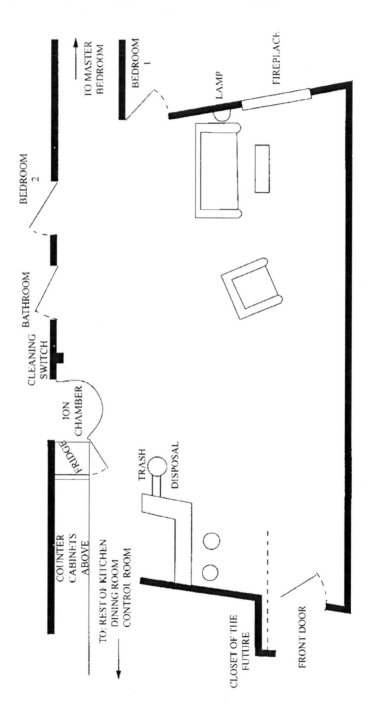

Also by
MICHAEL PARKER...

The Amorous Ambassador

Hotbed Hotel

The Lone Star Love Potion

The Sensuous Senator

There's a Burglar in My Bed

Who's in Bed with the Butler

Whose Wives Are They Anyway?

AND

Sin, Sex & the C.I.A.
by Michael Parker and Susan Parker

Please visit our website **samuelfrench.com** for complete
descriptions and licensing information

Printed in the United States
205194BV00011B/1-9/P